Churchill

BLOOD, SWEAT, & COURAGE

WWII CHRONICLES

Contents

50

First published in the UK in 2013

This edition published by Park Lane Books

www.parklanebooks.com

Printed in China

ISBN: 978-1-906969-45-5

Designed by: BrainWave

Creative Director: Kevin Gardner

Written by: Adam Powley

Images courtesy of Mary Evans Picture Library, PA Photos, Mirrorpix, and Wiki Commons

www.maryevans.com

Introduction

■ **ABOVE: Churchill pictured at his desk reading correspondence, 1933.**

"History will be kind to me for I intend to write it."

– Winston Churchill

Each historical era features its standout figures who transcend their age. The 20th century produced a long cast list of heroes and villains, larger-than-life personalities, and famous men and women who carved their name into history with their deeds in their own lifetime. And among that number, few made as much impact and left such a legacy as Winston Churchill.

Warrior, statesman, fighter, politician, troublemaker, writer, artist, drinker, curmudgeon, Nobel Prize winner, historian, maverick, and inspirational leader: Churchill was all these and much more. Of all the great leaders of the 20th century, few were as complex, complicated, and compelling as Winston Leonard Spencer Churchill.

Born as a son of the British Empire in the Victorian age and steeped in aristocratic traditions, he lived well into the latter half of the 20th century through a period when the world had been utterly transformed. He was central to the epochal changes and events within his long life, bestriding many of the greatest moments and themes of the modern period. In war and in peace he was a colossal figure – often controversial and not without opponents and enemies, but rarely out of the picture. Churchill dominated public life like few others, whether on the domestic or international stage.

A skip through his career reads like a timeline of major historical milestones: the Boer War, the First World War, revolution, the General Strike, the Great Depression, the Second World War, the decline of the British Empire, the Cold War, and the nuclear age. Churchill was there at almost every turn, impressing his beliefs, pursuing his strategy and policies, and shaping events on a global scale. He held high office in a variety of vaunted posts and even when he lost influence and official position, would not be cowed and was ever hungry for a comeback.

As a man, he was a bewildering mixture of often-conflicting characteristics. He was supremely

■ **ABOVE: An illustration of a young Churchill whilst operating as a Boer War correspondent.**

confident and determined but prone to introspection and wracked by spells of deep depression. He could be charming and wounding, generous and heartless, provocative, belligerent, manipulative. Churchill was often witty, readily gregarious, unpredictable, and often infuriating. He was a flawed and very human icon, whose strengths and weaknesses resulted in dazzling successes and humiliating failures. But in the

MR. WINSTON CHURCHILL

cutthroat game of politics and leadership, he stood out arguably unsurpassed in British history.

Churchill's childhood was often miserable and lonely, and he struggled at school. For all his high-society privileges, it took him three attempts to gain entry to the Royal Military College at Sandhurst. But once he enrolled and embarked upon the various strands of his career, he displayed a determination to succeed fueled by a burning desire to prove his worth. Ambitious for public office, he entered the world of politics with great gusto. His 60-year parliamentary career was never dull, often controversial, and unpredictable. His switch of party allegiance angered colleagues, and he could be reactionary yet also progressive in his outlook and actions.

For some observers he was dangerously reckless; others viewed him as courageously daring. He enjoyed mixed fortunes during and after the First World War and, at one stage, it seemed his high profile might be waning. But the resumption of conflict with the Second World War rekindled Churchill's fortunes and he seized the opportunity. He still had his adversaries and had to wage a hard battle to prevail, but once established as Prime Minister he rose to the task magnificently and rallied the British armed forces and its people. As the head of a national government, leading a country – and empire – fighting for its very survival, he combined a fierce will to win with extraordinary powers of oratory, clever diplomacy, and no little opportunism. It was the time and place Churchill had lived for and a role he seemed destined to fulfill.

Winning the war called for a pugnacious leader who could be ruthless when it counted and positive and optimistic when morale needed lifting. While others among the Establishment and elsewhere advocated appeasement, Churchill firmly rejected any such notions of defeatism. He bluntly offered "nothing but blood, toil, tears, and sweat" but his resolute leadership and uncompromising will to defend western interests and see Nazism vanquished was critical to the overall war effort. Civilization emerged from the horror of the Second World War brutally battered but alive, and Churchill had played a key part in ensuring its survival.

Yet, the world had changed and Churchill seemed yesterday's man. The British people acknowledged his supreme efforts but rejected him at the ballot box. For other men in their seventies, such a reversal would have ended their careers, but Churchill had come back before and would do so again, enjoying one last period of power.

His passing in 1965 at the grand old age of 90 was marked with a state funeral that seemed to draw a line under one era. Another, more high-tech age was already well into its stride by the time Churchill died, but he remained a figure of huge relevance for the post-war world. Even now, half a century after his death, he remains one of the most fascinating figures of modern history.

■ **OPPOSITE:** **Churchill pictured in 1940.**

■ **BELOW:** **A cartoon depiction of Winston Churchill, c.1913.**

Chapter One:

The Churchill Clan

■ **ABOVE: Churchill's family tree can be seen branching down from the 1st Duke of Marlborough, John Churchill, pictured here in a portrait at the Battle of Blenheim.**

"In all things but [my religion] the King may command me."

– John Churchill, 1st Duke of Marlborough

Sir Winston Churchill was favored, if not exactly destined, for greatness. His lineage was high ranking and part of the fabric of English aristocratic life and heritage. While his personal qualities, his drive, and fierce ambition of course determined his career to a fundamental extent, the connections and influences that stemmed from his background were an important factor in his rise to the pinnacle of political leadership. Churchill may not have enjoyed huge wealth relative to his contemporaries among the nobles of the land, and nor did he enjoy vaunted titles through inheritance, but he was bequeathed a family name that had fluctuating prominence in British history for over two centuries.

Not that such a standing necessarily translated into noble deeds and achievements for all the Churchills. Along the various strands of the family's genealogy there are a number of notable ancestral names, primarily Spencer, and also including Percy and Nevill. Some of those can be traced back to the time of William the Conqueror, as members of the Norman invasion force rewarded for their military support with land and title. Even so, not all of the descendants can be counted among the great, and certainly not the good.

Others in the Churchill family tree emerged as wealthy farmers, or movers and shakers within the perilous world of medieval power struggles. Churchill's forebears were there amid the religious tumult of the Reformation, the devastation of the English Civil War, and the dangerous religious rivalries of the Restoration and The Glorious Revolution of the late 17th century. Given the often bewildering complexity of inter-marriage and alliances forged between the various dynasties, links can be made with any number of distant relatives – Princess Diana, for example, whose maiden name was Spencer, is one of those with a Churchill association.

A clear family tree can be seen branching down from the 1st Duke of Marlborough, John Churchill. He was born in 1650 in Devon, England, the son of a Member of Parliament and drawn from among the English country gentry. While his origins were hardly humble compared to the vast majority of the population, his

subsequent career was based on his own ambition, an astute marriage choice, and, above all, his skill as a soldier and diplomat.

John Churchill became an officer at the age of 17 and rose rapidly through the ranks of command. He carefully negotiated his way through testing times at the royal court following the expulsion of James II as monarch, making an impressive comeback despite being ostracized by William III for three years, and even suffering a spell as a prisoner in the Tower of London. It was on the battlefield where Churchill really made his name, however.

In the late 17th and early 18th centuries, Britain was emerging as a European and world power, based on the strength of her navy and increasing economic strength, wielded across a growing empire – the empire of which Winston Churchill was such a staunch defender. His ancestor played a key role in ensuring that imperial strategy was able to flourish in the face of opposition from competing nations such as France, and John Churchill's contribution was acknowledged when he was made an earl in 1689.

On August 13, 1704, came the pivotal battle against the all-powerful French army and their Bavarian allies at Blenheim in southern Germany, during the War of the Spanish Succession. Churchill, by now enjoying the title of Duke of Marlborough, led a multi-national opposing force and, against the odds, recorded a decisive victory. It was triumphs such as these that have led many analysts to claim that Marlborough was the greatest of all English military commanders.

His stunning successes led a grateful monarchy to reward him with a grand palace, sited at Woodstock in Oxfordshire. Construction began in 1705 but was beset by financial troubles and

ABOVE: Sarah Jennings, the Duchess of Marlborough.

BELOW: Blenheim was the Churchill family seat for 300 years.

■ ABOVE: **John Winston Spencer, 7th Duke of Marlborough, was Winston's grandfather and a respected MP.**

the palace was only completed in 1733. Churchill's equally ambitious wife, Sarah Jennings, the Duchess of Marlborough, was scathing and called it a "pile of old stones," but its eventual grandeur was a clear illustration of her husband's rise to the "top-table" of British power and influence.

His descendants had a mixed record in making the most of their legacy. Blenheim would be the family seat for 300 years, but none of its occupants distinguished themselves to nearly the same extent that the man behind its foundation did – at least until Winston Churchill arrived.

Winston's grandfather, the 7th Duke,

was a respected MP representing the Woodstock constituency and served with some success in Benjamin Disraeli's governments. He was also Lord Lieutenant of Ireland from 1876 to 1880. The Duke's younger son, Lord Randolph, had clear ambitions to follow in his father's footsteps and exceed his achievements, but Randolph died at the age of just 45 (with remarkable coincidence, his son died on the same date in the calendar, January 24.)

Nonetheless, Lord Randolph was a key figure in the development of the movement called progressive Conservatism, otherwise known as "Tory Democracy," advocating the modernization of the party to appeal to and appease the growing working class. Randolph could be said to be moving with the times but he was constrained by the rules of an older era. As the third son of the Duke, his title of "Lord" was more of a temporary than permanent one, and as a result was not passed onto his own son Winston.

Lord Randolph's wife, and Winston's mother, was Jennie Jerome. As a daughter of rich American financiers and landowners, Jennie may have boasted membership of American high society and wowed England with her beauty – and her money was very welcome to a class of people that, for all their advantages, often failed to fully exploit inherited wealth. But, in the stuffy and snooty world of the English aristocracy, that counted for little in terms of "breeding." Thus, while her son Winston may have been born into a family with a rich aristocratic tradition, he was well removed from its more venerated and moneyed circles. Winston arrived at Blenheim, but was not, in the English phrase, "to the manor born." With such valuable family connections however, he was in a better position than most to realize his dreams.

ABOVE: **Lord Randolph Spencer Churchill (1849-1895).**

BELOW: **Jennie Jerome became Lady Randolph Churchill and was Winston's mother.**

Chapter Two:

Childhood

Winston Churchill entered a world dominated by the British Empire on November 30, 1874 (either two months premature or as a consequence of being conceived before his parents had married). With large slices of the global map colored pink to represent Britain's colonial rule, the infant Winston would grow up with a passionate commitment to preserving that power. It was a key facet of his ideals and personality. Winston's domestic upbringing was to naturally inform much of the rest of his character.

His formative experiences resulted in a strange mix of influences. The Churchills' aristocratic background ensured the family moved in the circles of "Society" – the insular, privileged, and powerful world of a handful of dynasties who had formed the nation's elites for centuries. Prime Ministers, judges, bishops, generals and admirals, mine owners, landowners, and the famous and acclaimed of the Victorian era were the people born to rule. They married into each other's families, strengthening the bonds of power and influence, and socialized with each other on the round of events and parties from racecourses to grand summer balls.

Yet, it was also a changing world and the Churchills were not in the middle of this circle. Winston himself would never be really rich and, as Geoffrey Best argues in *Churchill: A Study In Greatness*, as Churchill aged he moved further away from his noble heritage. During his childhood, by the standards of the day and their class, his family was not wealthy. Winston's father, Lord Randolph, had married Jennie partly out of

LEFT: Winston Churchill, aged five, in a sailor suit at his family home. At this time Churchill was living with his parents and grandparents at the Little Lodge, near the Viceregal residence in Dublin, 1879.

■ **ABOVE: Winston Churchill pictured with his mother Jennie and his brother John c.1886.**

practical need. As an American she was not from the English nobility but she had inherited wealth that her husband craved. It was a sign that the aristocracy's unquestioned ability to govern was being challenged and dependent on other means. Jennie's father reluctantly agreed to divide his daughter's allowance and she and Randolph were each given £1,000 a year.

With modest funding in place, Lord Randolph embarked on a political career that showed brief and spectacular promise before ending in disappointment and his early death in 1895. Syphilis was rumored to be the cause, though a brain tumor is more likely. At any rate, he was a distant figure and almost a stranger to his son Winston and his younger brother John, known as Jack. The latter was born in Dublin, where the family had moved when the boys' grandfather was appointed Viceroy of Ireland. Back in London, the family settled in St. James's Place, before Winston was, in common with so many of his peers, packed off at the age of eight to private school and the start of his education.

It was a sad and often miserable time in Churchill's life. His first school, St. George's, in Ascot, was an institution straight out of the stuff of English public school nightmares. Ruled with sadistic viciousness by the Reverend Herbert William Sneyd-Kynnersley, pupils were hectored into learning, with the constant threat of physical punishment looming over them. A school report from 1883 declared that Winston had "began term well but has latterly been very naughty." Retribution was swift and brutal, with floggings on bare behinds frequent. Compounded by the fact he was small in stature, often sickly, and

RIGHT: **Winston Churchill's school report commenting on his lateness and poor behaviour, c.1890.**

BELOW: **A smartly dressed Winston Churchill pictured when he was a schoolboy at Harrow, c.1889.**

"I keep Winston in good order as I know you like it. He is a clever boy and really not naughty but he wants a firm hand."
– the Duchess of Marlborough (Winston's grandmother), writing to his parents, 1888

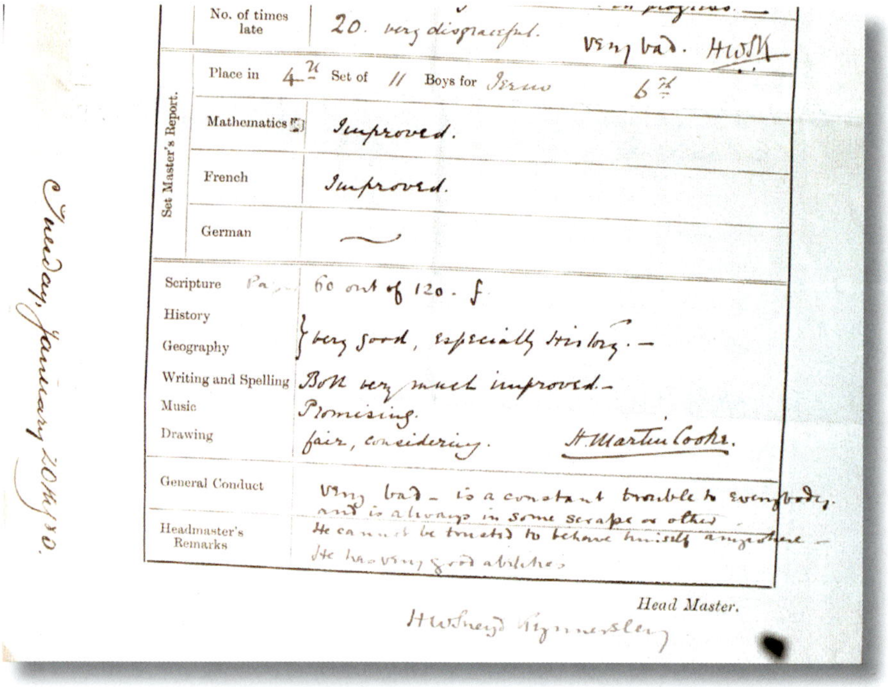

Tuesday, January 20th/90.

	No. of times late	20. very disgraceful. Very bad.
	Place in 4th Set of 11 Boys for Terms 6th	
Set Master's Report.	Mathematics	Improved.
	French	Improved.
	German	—
	Scripture	60 out of 120. f
	History / Geography	very good, especially History. –
	Writing and Spelling	Both very much improved. –
	Music	Promising.
	Drawing	fair, considering. H. Martin Cooke.
	General Conduct	Very bad – is a constant trouble to everybody and is always in some scrape or other.
	Headmaster's Remarks	He cannot be trusted to behave himself anywhere – He has very good abilities.

Head Master. H. W. Sneyd Kynnersley

had a speech impediment, Churchill had a hard time and his sufferings were considerable. Unsurprisingly, Churchill struggled with study and the experience no doubt contributed to his lasting limitations in formal educational achievement.

Looking back over a century later it seems cruel that his parents, and in particular his mother, could have condemned him to such treatment. It was an experience that was all too common at the time. Even for the age, however, it appears extreme and Jennie and Randolph rescued their son from St. George's and moved him to the more welcoming and enlightened Brunswick School in Hove.

Churchill's relationship with his mother was also by modern standards lacking in warmth and heartfelt affection. He wrote in his book, *My Early Life*, that she always seemed "like a fairy princess: a radiant being possessed of limitless riches and power. She shone for me like the Evening Star," though he tellingly added "I loved her dearly – but at a distance." This was the time of stiff-upper-lips and emotions kept in check, and expressions of genuine love were often rationed by parents toward their own young children.

Indeed, Jennie would come into her own in terms of supporting her son later in his life.

Yet Churchill did enjoy one childhood relationship that provided him with the kind of tender care, love, and attention that was lacking elsewhere. He grew very fond of his nanny and nurse, Elizabeth "Mrs." Everest, a kindly woman from the Medway towns of Kent and a place far removed from the gilded but cold world of high society. After his parents ended her employment – due to restricted finances – Winston maintained a close bond with Mrs. Everest (the "Mrs." was purely symbolic), who he called "Woom," and their letters, full of affectionate "darlings," "lovelys," and "kisses," spoke volumes. Following her death in 1895, Winston paid for her headstone and its upkeep for many years.

After Brunswick School, Winston was destined for one of the top public schools. Boys of his type either went to Eton or Harrow; Churchill was dispatched to the latter. The change in institution did little to alleviate Winston's discomfort with schooling. He begged his parents to visit him, often without the response he hoped for. His father would be busy in Parliament opposing plans to build a tunnel under the Channel rather than overly concern himself with his son's welfare. Jennie wrote to scold him for his lack of academic achievement. When he did write, Randolph could be spitefully hurtful. In one letter, he warned Winston of wasting his educational opportunities: "you will become a mere social wastrel, one of the hundreds of the public school failures, and you will degenerate into a shabby, unhappy and futile existence... I no longer attach the slightest weight to anything you say about your own acquirements and exploits."

Yet his son showed considerable promise in history and his character – bold (often cheeky), determined, and ready to fight his corner – was emerging. His English teacher, Robert Somervell, recognized promise in his pupil and the tutor's approach further encouraged Winston's development.

By the age of 15, it had been decided that the military would provide Winston's career path. He was enrolled in Harrow's "Army Class." Lord Randolph agreed with Winston's teachers that Woolwich, the officers' academy for the Royal Artillery and Royal Engineers, was beyond his son's mathematical ability so, Sandhurst, the academy for the infantry and cavalry, became the preferred option. Randolph had noticed Winston's enthusiasm for all things militaristic first hand when he had seen his collection of 1,500 toy soldiers lined up in battle order.

Playing soldiers for higher stakes proved more difficult. Winston twice failed the entrance exam to Sandhurst and had to be taught by Captain James, a "crammer" who got his pupil through the test with intensive individual study. In September 1893, Winston Churchill the schoolboy became Churchill, cavalry cadet.

■ **ABOVE: Churchill pictured in 1894 with two friends at Sandhurst, just before leaving to be commissioned in the 4th Royal Hussars.**

Chapter Three:

Churchill the Soldier

■ ABOVE: **Churchill in khaki service dress in Bangalore, India, 1897.**
■ OPPOSITE: **Churchill as a second lieutenant in the 4th Royal Hussars.**

"I am more ambitious for a reputation for personal courage than anything else in the world. A young man should worship a young man's ideals."

– Winston Churchill

Churchill spent 15 months at Sandhurst, and it is clear he enjoyed a more productive time than he ever did during the dispiriting years of his formal schooling. Army cadet life seemed to suit the increasingly ambitious young man and, having only just managed to gain entry to the academy, he flourished once in and left Sandhurst ranked among the highest in his peer group – eighth out of 150.

In the space of a little over two months, a number of significant events in his life occurred. First, Churchill left Sandhurst in December 1894. Then, in January 1895, Lord Randolph died. Winston's father had been ill for some time and, with trips abroad to try and remedy his poor health proving unsuccessful, he had returned to London to see out his last days. He died with much of his ambition unfulfilled – a poignant contrast with his son's growing determination to forge his own successful career.

By February, Winston was commissioned as a second lieutenant in the 4th Royal Hussars, a regiment with a long and distinguished place in the imperial military. Ironically, by excelling at Sandhurst, Churchill could have joined an infantry regiment, as his recently deceased father had wished. But his son chose to stand by his initial choice of serving with the cavalry.

Joining the army as a commissioned officer reflected Churchill's status but also masked his relative lack of wealth. His pay was £150 a year rising to £300 when posted to India. Given the cost of his horse and equipment, and his fondness for the good things in life, Churchill was short of funds, a fact which played a key impetus behind his search for work as a journalist and writer (see Chapter 4).

The posting to India was Churchill's first exposure to the

■ **ABOVE: Lord Kitchener was Churchill's commanding officer at the Battle of Omdurman.**

"jewel" in the British Empire's crown. His duties were limited and his time on the sub-continent was largely limited to run-of-the-mill tasks, training, trips to other regimental stations, and polo matches (the only team sport Churchill was really enthusiastic about and one in which he excelled). He did not let the time go to waste and, keen to make up for the shortcomings of his education, ploughed into books and scholarly reading. Yet for all his intellectual development, Churchill was unfulfilled and wrote that his time in India was largely "stupid, dull and uninteresting," fueling his impatience to see some proper action. A man of destiny such as Winston Churchill would not make his way in the world behind a desk or wasting his time in the officer's mess.

He got his wish to experience fighting for real in September 1897. By now a lieutenant, Churchill joined the Malakand Field Force in North West India, combining work as a correspondent with service on the commander's staff. Given his chance, the 22-year-old showed his mettle. In a scene straight out of stereotypical *Boy's Own* stories of British military pluck in the face of fierce aggression from marauding "natives," Churchill found himself in great peril, trapped by a tribal force in the Mamund Valley. Amid an intense firefight, he witnessed first hand the vicious realities of war, but he performed with conspicuous bravery. Churchill helped rescue a wounded soldier and might – perhaps should – have received a medal for his actions.

Given a taste of battle, Churchill relished more. He took part in further actions on the Northwest Frontier and was mentioned in dispatches. The stories of the fighting captivated the public back home, thanks to some gripping newspaper reports – some of them written by Churchill himself.

The eager officer next saw dangerous adventure in the Sudan in 1898, another of Britain's colonial theaters of war. Attached to the 21st Lancers under the leadership of General Kitchener in the Battle of Omdurman, Churchill took part in what may have been the last ever British cavalry charge. He paid his own way to Africa and, had he been killed, his family would have had to meet the costs of bringing his body back to Britain for burial. The risk of death and injury was very real indeed. Casualties were at their highest in the charge and Churchill had to fight desperately

using his revolver. He had dislocated his shoulder within moments of first arriving in India and as a result could not effectively use his sword.

While such experiences were what Churchill had craved, he was made brutally aware of the true cost of fighting for the glory and expansion of the Empire. While the British incurred fewer than 200 casualties, losses among the native Dervish force approached 10,000. It was an uneven slaughter resulting from a mismatch of weaponry, and Churchill did not shy from the harsh reality:

ABOVE: The Battle of Omdurman, 1898. The 21st Lancers delivered the last full-scale cavalry charge of modern warfare. (Purton Museum, England)

"The shoddiness of war. You cannot gild it. The raw comes through." Neither did he ignore the lesson that when one force has a combination of technological advantage, discipline, and effective training put into practice, it results in a potent and viciously effective means of victory on the battlefield.

By May 1899, Lieutenant Churchill had had his fill of fighting and resigned his commission. He had made a considerable mark in uniform, but now looked to further his ambitions in civilian attire.

Chapter Four:

Churchill the Journalist

ABOVE: Churchill pictured in 1895. Whilst on leave he developed an interest in journalism, writing about the conflict in Cuba.

"When first in the dim light of early morning I saw the shores of Cuba rise and define themselves from dark-blue horizons, I felt as if I sailed with Long John Silver and first gazed on Treasure Island... Here was a place where something would certainly happen. Here I might leave my bones."

– Winston Churchill

Life in the army had a doubly positive purpose for Winston Churchill. Not only did it enable him to spread his wings, see substantial chunks of the Empire, and forge a reputation for himself and his own ambitions, it also presented an opportunity to follow a more financially rewarding line of work. His inheritance was relatively meager and his mother, while providing good social connections and able to pull strings in his favor, could not adequately supplement his earnings as an officer. Writing for a living was an attractive proposition, and thus military service was to a significant extent inspired by his pursuit of a good story as a war correspondent.

Churchill got the journalistic bug in Cuba in 1895. Another European empire, this time the Spanish, was battling a rebellion in a far-flung colony. The Caribbean conflict would eventually drag America in and lead to the war of 1898, but three years earlier, thanks to introductory letters that impressed the Spanish authorities, Churchill managed to temporarily insert himself into the fighting against Cuban guerrillas along with his fellow officer, Lieutenant Reggie Barnes (who would go on to become General Sir Reginald Barnes). Both young men were seeking adventure away from the inertia of their everyday service, and took the chance to make the most of the five-month leave they were entitled to during the winter. There were even instructions from the British to gather military information, giving the trip a whiff of espionage. Churchill, however, had an added incentive, in the shape of a commission to write about the conflict for the illustrated London paper, the *Daily Graphic*.

After a stopover in New York that further fueled Churchill's growing admiration for American dynamism and democratic zeal, the pair arrived in Havana on November 20

ABOVE: A studio portrait of Churchill, taken shortly after his arrival in South Africa in 1899.

and a week later had joined up as observers with a government column led by General Valdez. The eight-day operation was Churchill's first experience of actual action and he came under fire on November 30. "[It] was my 21st birthday and on that day for the first time I heard shots fired in anger and heard bullets strike flesh or whistle through the air," he wrote.

While Churchill was in some danger, the fighting was piecemeal and more akin to skirmishing than actual battles, and so for all his breathlessly exciting writing, his bones were not to be left in the Caribbean. He and Barnes would receive medals for their limited service, the Cross of the Order of Military Merit and, in 1914, the Cuban Campaign Medal. Winston's time in Cuba had lasted 16 days. It gave him a lifetime love of Havana cigars and siestas, and inspiration for the writing of *Savrola*, his only work of fiction, that related a tale of popular rebellion against dictatorship – a narrative clearly influenced by his Cuban experiences.

The novel was written while Churchill was en-route to and back from India, and his enthusiasm for soldiering and reporting spurred him into further activity in fighting on the Northwest Frontier. His dispatches gave him a public profile as well as earning him much-needed income. He wrote articles for the *Daily Telegraph* (at £5 a time) and the *Allahabad Pioneer*. Once removed from the frontline he penned the book *The Story of the Malakand Field Force*, earning £600 for his efforts.

Exploits in the Sudan also provided Churchill with further writing opportunities. He reported for the *Morning Post*, again providing enthralled readers back in Britain with gripping stories of the Empire's soldiers in heroic action against what were regarded as savage natives. Winston knew full well what the reality was and was soon to leave the army. Back home in Britain, he began his two-volume work on the Sudan conflict, *The River War*, an acclaimed study that was subtitled "A Tale of Blood and War" – a telling reflection of the gory and costly nature of the fighting.

If Churchill had had his fill of seeing bloodshed, it was only temporary. Resigned from army service, he nonetheless still sought military adventure. The Second Boer War had an irresistible pull, for it was no ordinary colonial conflict between an invading white force and conquered indigenous peoples, but a bitter fight between a European power and its settlers against those of Dutch origin.

Having failed in his first attempt to become a Member of Parliament (see Chapter 5), Churchill headed to South Africa, reporting again for the *Morning Post* – this time at the rate of £250 per month for the four-month assignment, a considerable sum at that time. In mid-November 1899, he headed off by armored train to Ladysmith, British held and under

BELOW: Churchill in South Africa as a war correspondent for the *Morning Post* during the Boer War.

siege. In hostile territory the train came under attack from Boer fighters, and it was derailed. Churchill's soldierly instincts and training served him well, and he rallied nervous British troops but, after helping with the wounded and clearing the line, he and others were separated from the main force and captured.

Imprisoned in Pretoria with Captain Haldane, an old friend commanding the train, and a sergeant, the trio attempted escape but only Churchill was successful. Haldane later wrote of the action surrounding the train "Mr. Winston Churchill's conduct was that of as brave a man as could be found." This was little, however, compared to Churchill's miraculous escape from enemy territory. Slipping out of Pretoria, traveling incognito on trains, hiding in a mine, and avoiding recapture despite no knowledge of Afrikaans, he managed to reach Lourenco Marques, the capital of Portuguese East Africa, and safety.

By the time he reached Durban on December 23, he was a national hero back in Britain.

There would be further South African adventures. He re-enlisted with the South African Light Horse, and saw action in the major actions of Spion Kop, the relief of Ladysmith, Pretoria, and Johannesburg. He arranged for his brother Jack to be sent to the frontline and he was wounded while next to his elder brother. Winston himself managed to avoid injury yet, despite his repeated bravery, he did not receive the medals for gallantry he probably should have merited. He was not popular with the top brass, who disliked his notoriety and took exception to his criticism of their conduct of the war. Two more books were to follow: *London to Ladysmith*, recounting the armored train attack, and *Ian Hamilton's March*, which drew on his newspaper articles. Their 25-year-old author had recounted famous tales of derring-do but was now himself gaining increasing fame. The storyteller had become the story.

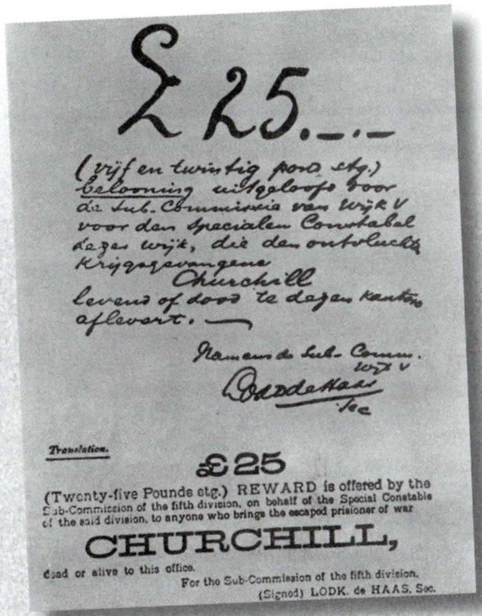

£25.–.–

(vijf en twintig pond stg.) belooning uitgeloofd voor de Sub-Commissie van Wijk V voor den Specialen Constabel dezer wijk, die den ontvluchte Krijgsgevangene
Churchill
levend of dood te dezen kantoor aflevert. —

Namens de Sub-Comm. Wijk V
Lodk de Haas
Sec.

Translation.

£25

(Twenty-five Pounds stg.) REWARD is offered by the Sub-Commission of the fifth division, on behalf of the Special Constable of the said division, to anyone who brings the escaped prisoner of war

CHURCHILL,

dead or alive to this office.

For the Sub-Commission of the fifth division.
(Signed) LODK. de HAAS, Sec.

■ **ABOVE:** **A "wanted" notice put out for Churchill after he escaped from a prisoner of war camp in South Africa during the Boer War. A reward was offered to anyone who brought the escaped prisoner dead or alive to the office.**

■ **BELOW:** **Churchill was a prisoner of war in Pretoria, South Africa, 1899.**

Chapter Five:

The Political Game

In tandem with his army and writing careers, Churchill was also busy seeking opportunities in the world of politics. His mother's impressive connections had helped smooth his progress in military service, and the vaunted social circles in which the family moved enabled her eldest son to meet and greet the great and the good of late-Victorian politics. Churchill sat down to dinner with such luminaries as Herbert Asquith and Arthur Balfour at an evening hosted by the hugely powerful Rothschild family. If young Winston was to successfully climb up the "greasy pole" of politics, he was going the right way about it in terms of connections.

His first opportunity to break into this world came with the Oldham by-election of 1899. This bustling town near Manchester had grown, thanks to the cotton industry, but retained a feature of the old British system of representation by electing two Members of Parliament. One of the Conservative Party's incumbents was ill; the other, Robert Ascroft, invited Churchill to stand as the other hopeful. In the event, Ascroft died, leaving Churchill to stand as the senior candidate, but without success.

BELOW: Churchill addressing a crowd in Hollinwood, Oldham, during the by-election of 1899.

Undaunted by this setback, Churchill returned to Oldham in 1900 for the General Election. He had impressed with his energy in the unsuccessful by-election a year before and, with his new fame as a hero of the Boer War, he was becoming more electable. Finishing second in the four-way tussle for the two seats, Winston Spencer Churchill became "W.S. Churchill – M.P."

Straight after, he headed off on a lucrative speaking tour of Britain and North America. The 26-year-old was a Conservative, but not a committed loyalist. He made his maiden speech in the House of Commons just four weeks after the death of Queen Victoria. Churchill was a politician for a new age. Political lines at the time were often blurred and ill-defined – Churchill first sought election in 1899 alongside a fellow Tory candidate who also headed a trade union.

While Churchill was a fierce defender of the Empire, led by a ruling class of which he was a member, and a staunch opponent of socialism (he would be labeled in some quarters as an "enemy of the working class"), Winston was nonetheless open to ideas. He was influenced by Seebohm Rowntree's *Poverty: A Study of Town Life*, and

became an advocate for social reform. This, and his support for free trade and criticisms of the government's military policy, put him at odds with Tory leaders and precipitated his departure from the party in 1904 to join the Liberals – literally crossing the Commons floor to take his place next to future Prime Minister, David Lloyd George.

This switch earned Churchill predictable accusations of treachery, but it did not harm his political progress. He was rewarded with appointment as Under-Secretary of State for the Colonies, and in the

"This small reverse will have no permanent ill effect on your political fortunes."
– Arthur Balfour, on Churchill's first election defeat

■ **BELOW: Now Under-Secretary of State for the Colonies, Churchill arrives at 10 Downing Street with John Morley, Secretary of State for India.**

1906 General Election Churchill took the seat of North West Manchester. Under Henry Campbell Bannerman and then Asquith, Churchill became one of the rising stars of Parliament, winning promotion to the cabinet as President of the Board of Trade, at a time when the Liberal government was legislating some key social reforms, from working hours to the setting up of Labor Exchanges to aid the unemployed, and the introduction of the famous "People's Budget" of 1909.

While keen to preserve the social order of Britain and the Empire, Winston was a modernizer and recognized the need to adapt. He could still be perceived as a traditionalist reactionary, however. When he became Home Secretary in 1911, his handling of a strike in the Welsh coalfields and subsequent industrial disputes earned him criticism from both sides – from union sympathizers angered at Churchill's role in the use of troops in strikes, to right-wing critics who felt he had not been tough enough.

There is continuing debate as to Churchill's true intentions during the Welsh dispute, but more visible were his actions during the infamous Sidney Street siege that began on January 2, 1911. Three weeks before, police had intercepted a group of robbers breaking into a jeweler's shop in Houndsditch on the edge of the City of London. A gun battle broke out in which three police officers were killed, and the gang's leader, Poloski Morountzeff, a Latvian, was mistakenly shot in the back by one of his accomplices.

Rumors swirled that the gang was a group of Jewish Eastern European anarchists. London and particularly the East End at the time were plagued by anti-Semitism against the Jewish immigrant community, while the Establishment was terrified of the menace of armed revolutionaries. When police received a tip-off that the remaining gang members were holed up in a house in Sidney Street, the tension was broken by a violent and fatal siege.

With a crowd of excited onlookers gathering and abuse shouted out against immigrants, Churchill arrived from Westminster to oversee operations at the scene. As troops were deployed, the Home Secretary, resplendent in his top hat, was captured by a photographer. Archive footage shows Churchill peering around from the protection of a corner as volleys of fire were exchanged. Eventually, after one particularly noisy fusillade, the house caught fire. Churchill supported the decision not to let the fire brigade in to dowse the flames and rescue the gang members. Two were later found dead in the charred building.

The siege was an example of Churchill's ability to put himself front of stage in a national drama. He had met, wooed, and wedded his wife Clementine in 1908, but marriage did nothing to diminish his growing impression on public life. Winston was soon to seek and gain higher office.

Chapter Six:

First Lord of the Admiralty

> *"So now the Admiralty wireless whispers through the ether to the tall masts of ships, and captains pace their decks absorbed in thought."*
> **– Winston Churchill**

■ **ABOVE: Winston Churchill and Clementine Hozier married on September 12, 1908.**

Churchill's first meeting with the woman who was to become his wife did not suggest they would spend their lives in happily married bliss. "He never uttered a word," recalled Clementine, in 1908 known as Miss Clementine Hozier. "He never asked me to dance, he never asked me to have supper with him – he just stood and stared." For once, Winston may have been speechless, but he was captivated by Clementine and they formed an enduring and very loving partnership that lasted 57 years.

They had five children. Diana (born 1909); Randolph (1911); Sarah (1914). Their fourth was Marigold who tragically died at the age of three from septicemia. Remarkably, "Clemmie" had offered her daughter to her close friend Lady Hamilton (wife of Winston's own close friend Sir Ian), in sympathy for the couple's inability to have their own children. The Churchills' fifth child, Mary, was born in 1922.

Life for Clementine with her husband was never dull and often testing. But in public she was known for her cool head and wise counsel. Both came in useful during her husband's tempestuous spell as First Lord of the Admiralty, the senior position on the Board of Admiralty that ran the Royal Navy. Winston was appointed in October 1911 with a clear brief, and he committed himself to the task with much energy and enthusiasm. He was a soldier at heart but the navy provided him with the position of high office he craved and the opportunity to affect real influence on a global scale.

The navy he inherited was still regarded as the most powerful ocean-borne force in the world but faced considerable challenges. Strength at sea had underpinned Britain's rise and the building of empire, but time had caught up. Other nations such as Japan and the United States had vast fleets of their own – Germany likewise. A country only unified in 1871 was now posing a serious threat to peace and stability in Europe. The German army was increasing in size and potential and so too her navy with the deployment of ships boasting the latest in naval technology.

The Royal Navy, by contrast, was stuck in a time warp. It hadn't fought a concerted war for 50 years and was staffed by admirals resistant to change and any challenge to their established ways. Britain did, just about, still rule the waves, but the grip on power was slipping. The Royal Navy was in some respects still "Nelson's Navy" and what it lacked in modern leadership was compounded by outdated and obsolete ships.

Any change was always going to meet opposition and Churchill certainly ruffled feathers, but once installed at the Admiralty, he revitalized and modernized the "senior service." New ships were built, including battleships with the biggest guns that could be deployed. Training was overhauled, promotion based on merit encouraged, and there was a general improvement in conditions for all ranks. Churchill also instigated the Royal Naval Air Service – a move which raised many eyebrows at the time but which was typically farsighted. Another key change was to switch Royal Navy ships from using coal as a power source to oil. To this end, Churchill pressed the government to secure fuel supplies by heavily investing in the Anglo-Persian Oil Company, which would evolve into British Petroleum.

Winston commented that his spell as First Lord of the Admiralty was his most enjoyable in senior office. He could be frustrating to deal with, dogmatic, over reaching, and very rude, but his persistence and vitality was what was required.

August 15, 1914] THE SPHERE 183

The MEN who are DIRECTING BRITAIN'S NAVY.

DRAWN BY F. MATANIA

THE FIRST LORD WITH HIS TWO HIGHEST EXECUTIVE OFFICERS

RIGHT HON. WINSTON CHURCHILL—Mr. Churchill is not quite forty years old yet, but he is known throughout the world as a most capable administrator of English affairs. He was first elected for Parliament in 1900 as a Conservative member, but in the year 1906 he was returned for N.W. Manchester as a Liberal. He has been First Lord of the Admiralty since 1911

REAR-ADMIRAL CHARLES MADDEN (second in command) has just relinquished the command of the 3rd Cruiser Squadron of the Home Fleets. He entered the Navy in 1875. He was in command of one of the earliest flotillas of torpedo-boat destroyers in the Mediterranean. He became captain of the original "Dreadnought" in 1907. He has gained a high reputation

ADMIRAL SIR JOHN JELLICOE—Vice-Admiral Jellicoe has just been appointed Commander-in-Chief of the Home Fleet in place of Admiral Callaghan. Admiral Jellicoe has acted since 1912 as Second Sea Lord of the Admiralty. He saw service in China from 1898-1901, when he commanded the Naval Brigade there. He was commander of the Atlantic Fleet during 1910-11

■ **LEFT: Discussing strategy with two senior naval commanders – Madden and Jellicoe.**

■ **BELOW: Churchill is seen here in his role as First Lord of the Admiralty, inspecting sailors at Chatham.**

War was looming and Churchill saw clearer than most of how grave the threat was.

There were also domestic challenges to deal with. The issue of home rule for Ireland was always a contentious one, leading to poisonous enmities and the near-impossible task of resolving a bitter issue formed over centuries of colonial rule. Churchill may still have been a devoted supporter of the Empire but he favored home rule, thus further fueling the ire of his opponents. After the Third Home Rule Bill was passed in 1912, the reaction in the north amongst protestant unionists turned violent.

This opposition was halted (temporarily) by the advent of war on a far larger scale. Tensions on the continent had been building and reached a turning point in the Balkans when Archduke Franz Ferdinand of Austria was assassinated in Sarajevo on June 28, 1914, by a Croatian nationalist called Gavrilo Princip.

The "shot that rang around the world" set off a chain-reaction of alliances and agreements between competing European powers, and was to drag in nations from as far afield as Canada and China.

On August 3, 1914, Sir Edward Grey, head of the British Foreign Office, was watching London's street lamps being lit. His comment that "the lamps are going out all over Europe; we shall not see them lit again in our lifetime," resonated with the terrible prospect of what horrors lay in store. At the time, millions enthusiastically signed up for service in the mistaken belief it would "all be over by Christmas." Churchill had seen more than most what the reality of war was like and was under few illusions. A day after Grey's solemn observation, the order was issued to "Commence hostilities against Germany" to all Royal Navy ships.

Churchill entered the fray with great gusto. He set up the Admiralty War Group, with himself firmly in control. There were early setbacks with the navy operating a blockade but unable to prevent attacks on commercial shipping. Churchill would not be constrained by the limits of war at sea, however, and was keen to have his say to Lord Kitchener on how the army should be run as well.

Winston nearly came unstuck, however, during the attempt to safeguard the strategically vital port of Antwerp in October 1914. As a firm advocate of sending considerable force to protect the port, Churchill traveled to Antwerp and even offered to resign his ministerial post in order to take command of Allied troops in the area. The advance of German forces and their powerful artillery, however, ended such grand ideas. Churchill left the city the day before the city surrendered.

It led to severe criticism and mockery. Churchill had made further enemies and enraged those who had long opposed him – but a greater setback was in store.

Chapter Seven:

Gallipoli, Disgrace, and Comeback

LEFT: Admiral and Sea Lord of the Royal Navy John Fisher, who Churchill brought back out of retirement.

RIGHT: General Sir Ian Standish Monteith Hamilton GCB GCMG DSO TD, most notably known for commanding the ill-fated Mediterranean Expeditionary Force during the Battle of Gallipoli.

Undaunted by the setback at Antwerp, Churchill sought to ensure he had a prominent place in the government's conduct of the conflict. He had served on the War Council and, despite the scathing reaction to his antics in Belgium, was brimming with confidence and self-belief. As an indication of his control, he brought Admiral John "Jackie" Fisher out of retirement to work alongside him as First Sea Lord.

Churchill then turned his attention to opening up new fronts in the war. With the Allies bogged down in France and Belgium, Churchill proposed an assault in other theaters to stretch the forces of the German-led Central Powers, and to encourage new combatants to come into the war on the side of the Allies. He cast his eyes on the Mediterranean and Turkey, the center of the Ottoman Empire. While this world power was in decline after centuries of holding significant sway over parts of Europe and the Middle East, it still presented formidable opposition. The promise of a victory over the Turks was very tempting. If the Allies could defeat or sideline Turkey they could open up a supply route through the Dardanelles and on to the Black Sea to aid the Russians fighting alongside Britain and France. The southern flank of Germany and Austria-Hungary would also be threatened.

In November 1914, Churchill laid out his plans and the operation was given the go ahead. A naval attack through the Dardanelles began in February 1915, but after initial success the assault was severely hampered by mines. The Admiralty had sent in old and outdated battleships rather than risk their more valuable modern vessels, but even the loss of these ships forced a revision in the plan. The Allies had hoped to avoid the use of ground troops, but began long preparations to land a sizable force, commanded by Churchill's old friend General Sir Ian Hamilton and including two divisions of Australian and New Zealand troops.

The extended preparations for the landing enabled the Ottoman defenders to regroup and rearm on the Gallipoli peninsula. By the time Allied troops made beach landings on April 25, the enemy was dug in and able to repel the invasion, pinning the Allied soldiers on the beaches and hillsides, and inflicting terrible losses.

Churchill had hoped to avoid the bloody stalemate of the Western Front. Instead, Gallipoli turned into equally savage and static trench warfare either under a merciless summer sun, or, in the later stages of the campaign, debilitating rain and cold. The suffering on both sides was horrendous and, by the beginning of

■ BELOW: **British troops advance on mass up the cliffs at Gallipoli off the Dardanelles straits. "Short of ammunition but still they press on, the true bulldog rush of our troops."**

the winter, Allied casualties amounted to over 200,000 men. The decision was made to evacuate. Gallipoli had been a disaster.

Predictably, there were major repercussions. Fisher and Churchill were two combustible personalities and they clashed from the outset. After a row over the drain on Royal Navy resources, Fisher resigned as early as May. Ian Hamilton's career was also over. On the political side, Churchill was in the firing line and it was his aggrieved enemies who had him in their sights. A crisis in the government let party and personal differences loose. Asquith's administration collapsed and a new coalition was eventually headed by Winston's political mentor and ally, David Lloyd George. In the meantime, the Conservatives made it a condition that Churchill was not in cabinet. Instead, he was given the post of Chancellor of the Duchy of Lancaster, a comparatively meaningless position.

It was a humiliating reverse. Recognizing the reality of his status, Winston resigned and rejoined the British army. He briefly commanded a battalion of the Royal Scots Fusiliers as a colonel without seeing much in the way of action. Even when Lloyd George restored Churchill to the cabinet in mid-1917, it was as Minister of Munitions, and not as one of the inner circle of senior politicians determining the conduct of the war.

"I thought he would die of grief," said Clementine years later of this period of ignominy. Yet her husband was far from finished and Lloyd George promoted him to Minister of War and Air in 1919, then Colonial Secretary in 1921. It was a controversial period: Churchill was widely criticized for his support for bombing rebellious tribesmen in Iraq. He even suggested the use of chemical weapons against "uncivilized" tribes people – combatants or not – illustrating his more repressive and vicious instincts against indigenous people who happened to get in the way of the British Empire. Such views were fueled by the fear of revolution and a challenge to established ways: Churchill was a fierce opponent of the Russian Revolution.

ABOVE: **Winston, his wife Clementine, and their daughter Sarah, at the top of the Mall in 1919, when they watched troops of the Brigade of Guards in a march past.**

OPPOSITE: **Churchill walks into the House of Commons during the General Strike.**

There was controversy of a familiar Churchillian kind back home when he was defeated in the 1922 General Election, losing his seat in

Dundee – and also his appendix after an operation. Winston won the constituency of Epping in the snap election of 1924 and performed another U-turn, by rejoining the Conservatives. "Anyone can rat, but it takes a certain ingenuity to re-rat," was his response to the inevitable anger of colleagues and foes.

Within a year, he was back in ministerial office under Prime Minister Stanley Baldwin. As Chancellor of the Exchequer, he returned Britain to the Gold Standard in the face of significant opposition and took an overall hard line during the General Strike of 1926, which was a direct consequence of his economic policy. He also spoke in admiration of Benito Mussolini amid the rise of Fascism in Italy. The eager social reformer of the Edwardian era, who wished to improve the condition of the working man, was prone to actions and pronouncements that cast him as a reactionary and outdated extremist.

Indeed, it looked as if his career would end on a sour and defeated note in 1929, when, amid the turmoil of the Great Depression, he was ousted from his office as the Tories lost the General Election, and was then passed over two years later when Ramsay MacDonald formed the National Government.

Cast out from the heart of politics, Winston was about to enter what were called the wilderness years.

"Are there not other alternatives than sending our armies to chew barbed wire in Flanders?"
– Winston Churchill

Chapter Eight:

Out in the Wilderness

The period between 1929 and 1939 may well have been a decade when Winston Churchill was removed from the center of politics and international affairs, but he did not spend it in quiet and inactive isolation.

He was, however, increasingly isolated from the mainstream in terms of policy. His lasting opposition to trade tariffs put him at loggerheads with the Conservative leadership, while his conduct over the issue of India seeking dominion status further alienated him from the consensus. Even some of Britain's most stalwart defenders of empire realized that the colonies had a right to become independent, but Churchill was not among them.

He was one of the founders of the India Defence League, which directly opposed government moves to accede to some of the wishes of the Indian nationalist movements. Churchill was scathing and gratuitously nasty about Mohandas Ghandi and expressed a lasting, cynical, and often vicious disregard for subjugated peoples. "It is alarming and also nauseating to see Mr. Gandhi," Churchill infamously said, "a seditious Middle Temple lawyer, now posing as a fakir of a type well-known in the East, striding half-naked up the steps of the Vice-regal palace... to parley on equal terms with the representative of the King-Emperor."

Churchill had a highly traditional view of hierarchy and social order and the empire's relationship to that order. He believed in the improvement in the condition of the "lower classes" but believed it best served by maintaining society's structure, not revolutionizing it (he even floated the idea of re-establishing the vote based on property). To modern minds some of Churchill's views are extreme and often racist, though it should be noted they were not uncommon at the time. Yet his position then put him on the margins of national and international politics.

■ **BELOW: Churchill on horseback during a visit to Banff, in the Canadian Rockies, 1929.**

Churchill found more gainful activity in his writing. He wrote a biography of the 1st Duke of Marlborough, began his epic *A History of the English-Speaking Peoples*, and went on speaking and writing tours to America. He would work late into the night dictating to secretaries and talking at length to his researcher, Maurice Ashley. He wrote extensively for the press and would be paid about £400 for an article, and once claimed he earned £20,000 a year from his journalism and book writing.

The family needed the money. Churchill bought Chartwell in 1922, despite Clementine's misgivings. Always concerned about the family's precarious finances given her husband's taste for high living, she feared the house would be a drain on resources and was proved right. But the house, with its commanding views of Kent countryside, was Winston's domain and he poured many hours into its restoration and expansion. During many convivial dinners and meetings he also poured plenty into his whiskey, sherry, and champagne glasses, but he could hold his drink.

He even built many of the walls in the ground of Chartwell himself – bricklaying may have been an odd hobby for a descendant of the Dukes of Marlborough, but he found the

■ **ABOVE: Chartwell was the country home of Churchill. He bought it in 1922.**

■ **BELOW: Winston Churchill leaves 10 Downing Street after meeting with British Prime Minister Neville Chamberlain in London, 1938.**

activity rewarding, allowing him time for contemplation and relief from the periods of depression he called his "black dog." The extent of his mental debilitation became clearer after his death but, while these episodes were serious, they did not hinder his work rate or lasting ambition.

Chartwell gave him a base from which to exercise some kind of power. He retained a circle of notable and powerful friends and acquaintances in high places who were frequent visitors, including the newspaper magnate Lord Beaverbrook, Lloyd George, and T.E. Lawrence (of Arabia fame). Chartwell may have been Churchill's country seat but it was just an hour's drive from central London. Winston kept close to the seat of power even if he wasn't quite in it.

Controversy was rarely far from Churchill's door, however. During the abdication crisis of 1936, when King Edward VIII announced his intention to marry an American divorcee, Wallis Simpson, Winston took the contrary view and supported the monarch, rather than the Prime Minister and the main parties who opposed the marriage on constitutional grounds. It set Churchill against public opinion and even he admitted his political career might have been finished.

But already there was one issue in which, far from being behind the times, Churchill was way ahead. As early as 1932 he warned of the dangers of German rearmament. While he continued to write and speak against communism and anti-imperial movements, he recognized the growing threat of Adolf Hitler and Nazism. This was a testing and difficult period. Economic strife, political extremism at home, civil war in Spain, and wars elsewhere around the world created a worrying expectation of another global conflict that many were, understandably, desperate to avoid.

Churchill knew all too well what war entailed. He wrote in his 1930 book, *My Early Life*, "In contrast with my school days, I had made many friends, three or four of whom still survive. As for the rest they are gone. The South African War accounted for a large proportion not only of my friends but of my company, and the Great War killed almost all the others. The few that survived have been pierced through thigh or breast or face by the bullets of the enemy." But Churchill also recognized the threat Germany posed and, at a time when so many wished to appease Hitler, he was outspoken in his opposing view. In a memorable response to Neville Chamberlain in September 1938, he said of the Prime Minister's supposed pact with Hitler "You were given the choice between war and dishonor. You chose dishonor, and you will have war."

Churchill's warning was about to come true.

"I have taken more out of alcohol than alcohol has taken out of me."
– Winston Churchill

Chapter Nine:

Winston is Back

ABOVE: Prime Minister Neville Chamberlain makes his famous "Peace in Our Time" speech upon returning from talks with German Chancellor Adolf Hitler in Munich. Within a year, Britain was at war with Germany.

Hitler's promises to Neville Chamberlain were as hollow as any number of his assurances to the people of Europe and beyond that he had no ambitions to carve out a new world order through force and war. The piece of paper that Chamberlain flourished on his return from Munich as a guarantee of "peace in our time" was worthless – Hitler himself dismissed it as a "scrap" – and with the invasion of Poland the lies and double crosses were finally exposed. Appeasement had not worked. Churchill had been proved right.

Though rearmament and modernization of the armed forces had begun, Britain lagged way behind Germany. What was immediately needed was a rapid commitment to placing industry on a war footing and men experienced in government during conflict. For all his faults, flaws, and previous mistakes, Churchill fitted the bill. On September 3, 1939, the day war was declared, Winston was brought in from the wilderness to his old post as First Lord of the Admiralty. He sent word that he would be in his office at 6pm. Every ship in the navy received the signal "Winston is back."

He wasted little time in making his mark. While the "phoney war" lulled many into a false sense of security, Churchill pushed (in vain) for the occupation of strategically vital Scandinavian ports. Instead, Germany successfully invaded Norway. The setback contributed to a withering lack of confidence in Chamberlain who was seen as weak and indecisive. By contrast, Churchill was viewed as a man of ideas and action. On April 4, 1940, he became chairman of the Military Coordinating Committee; a month later he landed the big job. Without support in the House, a weary and defeated Chamberlain resigned on May 10. The same day, the King called on Churchill to form a government, with Winston as its Prime Minister.

Forty years after he had first entered Parliament, Churchill secured the great office he had dreamed of, but in nightmarish circumstances. With Western Europe capitulating in the face of the Blitzkrieg tactics of the German war machine, Britain was left standing virtually alone. France fell in just over a month. The disaster at Dunkirk, in which over 300,000 Allied soldiers were rescued, might have been miraculous, but it was, in truth, a humiliating defeat. The invasion of Britain seemed inevitable, and key and influential figures began to advocate a peace accord with Nazism.

Now Churchill came into his own. While in private he half joked about being dead within three months, publicly he provided a resolute, inspirational example of good old-fashioned British pluck and a refusal to surrender to tyranny.

He was an unlikely leader to rally behind. Churchill *was* a unifying figure: he was despised by politicians across the political divide, and no more so than in the Conservative Party. Yet the sense of right time, right place, right man, rings true. Churchill's energy, single-minded determination, his reputation as an unpredictable maverick, and his gift for lyrically articulating high-minded aims was not best suited to peace time but just what was required in war. He brought in politicians from all parties. Tory MPs who had once harangued him now cheered him. Left-wingers who hated his interwar policies rallied to the cause.

Churchill's speech-making was fundamental to his new-found popularity. He always had a gift of rhetoric – now it was put to devastatingly impressive use. In his first speech as Prime Minister he offered nothing "but blood, toil, tears, and sweat." On June 4, with Luftwaffe

ABOVE: First Lord of the Admiralty Winston Churchill leaves his home in London to travel to the Admiralty, September 3, 1939.

"I displayed the smiling confidence and confident air which are thought suitable when things are very bad."
– Winston Churchill, *The Second World War*

planes poised to unleash terror on British soil, he said "we shall defend our island, whatever the cost may be, we shall fight on the beaches, we shall fight on the landing grounds, we shall fight in the fields and in the streets, we shall fight in the hills; we shall never surrender."

It was historic, intense oratory that helped transform Churchill into a national hero and begin the legend of Winston the war leader. It was only the start. June 18 saw perhaps his most eloquent and moving speech yet. Again, he combined beautiful

■ **LEFT: An interior view of the Free Trade Hall building in Peter Street, Manchester, showing the packed out hall gathered to hear the speech of First Lord of the Admiralty Winston Churchill where he declared, "each to our station... there is not a week, nor a day, nor an hour to be lost," 1940.**

wordplay with assertions that cut to the heart of the conflict and Britain's place in it. "Let us therefore brace ourselves to our duties, and so bear ourselves, that if the British Empire and its Commonwealth last for a thousand years, men will still say, 'this was their finest hour'."

The speech came as the RAF fought a desperate struggle to deny the Luftwaffe command of the skies. What was at stake was nothing less than survival. Britain faced an evil enemy unprecedented in history. The two leaders now pitted against each other symbolized that struggle. Hitler and Churchill never met, though they came close in 1932 when Churchill visited Munich. While Hitler was an admirer of the way the British had established the empire that Churchill always sought to defend, the pair were ideologically opposed. Churchill knew what victory for Nazism entailed. Now he led the battle to ensure that horrific outcome was prevented.

■ **RIGHT: Churchill tries a Tommy gun during a visit to northeast England, to inspect coastal fortifications and defense works. The background behind Churchill has been blotted out by the censor, 1940.**

Chapter Ten:

The Darkest Hours

■ **ABOVE: A Nazi Heinkel 111 bomber flies over London during the Battle of Britain in the fall of 1940 during the Second World War. The River Thames runs through the center.**

The Battle of Britain was one of the most pivotal events of the whole of the Second World War and provided the sternest of tests for the man who had only recently been installed as Prime Minister. With Britain all but alone in facing the might of German land armor, naval strength, and air power, Churchill's call to arms was unequivocal.

His gift for rhetoric had already been employed to lay out in uncompromising terms the need for sacrifice while offering nothing more in return than "blood, toil, tears, and sweat." His call for his Britons to "fight on the beaches" stirred an island nation fearful of invasion and conquest. The visionary ambition that, in some point in the future, the outcome of the conflict would be seen as the nation's "finest hour" provided a ray of hope in the darkest of times. But, with the Luftwaffe raining death and destruction on British cities and industry, the need for Churchill's inspirational speech-making was needed more than ever.

Early probing raids through late June and into July had given way to more concerted attacks on shipping, ports, and harbors. But the resistance of the RAF's embattled Fighter Command, led by Sir Hugh Dowding, had inflicted a stiff response to German aggression. While the RAF operated on a knife edge, battling against a drain on the precious number of pilots and aircraft, Fighter Command was able to inflict greater damage on the Luftwaffe's bombers and fighters.

By the beginning of August, the focus of the battle shifted. Recognizing that command of the air was a prerequisite before any seaborne invasion of the British mainland, Hitler had ordered a switch in tactics to eliminating RAF airfields, command centers, and radar installations. Hermann Göring, as over-confident as ever, assured the Fuhrer he could knock out Fighter Command's 10 and 11 groups within four days and the whole of the RAF within a month.

ABOVE: Sir Hugh Dowding GCVO KGB CMG, the man in charge of Britain's fighter defenses during the Battle of Britain.

BELOW: Hermann Göring speaks during the air battle for England with a pilot who returned from the enemy flight.

"Destroy the English air force as soon as possible."
– Adolf Hitler's command to Göring

Göring had not reckoned for the tenacity, supreme expertise, and utmost courage of Fighter Command's pilots, however. Drawn from a number of nationalities and backgrounds, these young men, supported by their hardworking ground crews, together with other men and women who served across RAF operations, turned Churchill's stirring words into real-life action.

It was a desperate struggle, incurring appalling losses on both sides in a conflict both sides were desperate to win but, knowing what was at stake, the RAF began to overcome the odds and gain the upper hand. "Members of the RAF – the fate of generations lies in your hands," was the command order, and the pilots followed the instruction with incredible courage.

The Germans dubbed August 15 "Black Thursday," in recognition of severe losses amid the most intense raids of the battle so far. They were not the only ones struck by the RAF's capabilities. The next day, Churchill visited Air-Vice Marshal Keith Park's 11 Group HQ at Uxbridge. Seeing first hand the scale of activity and hearing via radio the voices of pilots engaged in bitter dogfights made a profound impression on the Prime Minister.

In the journey back to London, Churchill was markedly quiet. "Don't speak to me," he said to his secretary, Major General Ismay. "I have never been so moved in my whole life." The silence was broken when Churchill added, "Never in the field of human conflict was so much owed by so many to so few."

It has been claimed that Churchill actually said "never in the field of human history," and that Ismay responded by suggesting "human

■ **ABOVE: The wreckage of a home "somewhere in England" the London censor approved caption said, as German air attacks reached inside the coast, August 15, 1940. Note the undamaged air-raid shelter in the right background.**

conflict" was more appropriate. Whatever the truth of the story, it is clear that the experience at Uxbridge would have a significant – even historic – effect on the course of Britain's conduct through the war and arguably beyond.

On August 20, 1940, Churchill took to his feet in the House of Commons to deliver a speech that both defined his power of oratory and Britain's character in the war, and in the post-war era. It was an extensive address that veered from the relatively mundane to subjects of world-shaping significance. There were reports of aircraft and armament production, and even a comment about how potatoes could be used as fuel by fermenting and distilling them into alcohol spirit.

Churchill was reflecting on the passage of the war thus far. By no means was every MP in the House happy with his conduct as Britain's war leader. Always a divisive character, Churchill had many opponents – and even allies – who viewed his actions and motives with suspicion. Nonetheless, he had been well received when he rose to the dispatch box – but, as the speech progressed, his combination of confidence, determination, and moving testimony earned loud approval. He was cheered for his rallying cries; his mockery of Hitler and the Third Reich prompted loud and welcome laughter. But it was in his tribute to the RAF that Churchill really found the power to energize, inspire, and move his audience – not just the gathered MPs but also the millions who later listened to the speech re-recorded for the BBC.

"The great air battle," Churchill solemnly announced, "which has been in progress over this island for the last few weeks has recently attained a high intensity. It is too soon to attempt to assign limits either to its scale or to its duration. We must certainly expect that greater efforts will be made by the enemy than any he has so far put forth."

In countering those efforts, the RAF had delivered a bloody retort to Hitler's ambitions. Churchill continued: "The gratitude of every home in our island, in our Empire, and indeed throughout the world, except in the abodes of the guilty, goes out to the British airmen who, undaunted by odds, unwearied in their constant challenge and mortal danger, are turning the tide of the World War by their prowess and by their devotion.

"Never in the field of human conflict was so much owed by so many to so few."

It was spine-tingling speech-making, instantly capturing the spirit of collective defiance, while bolstering morale. Churchill had an abiding conviction from the outset of the conflict that the war could be won. He had a huge task in persuading a brave but also fearful nation that the Nazis could be defeated. "The Few" speech was a fundamental example of Churchill's ability to communicate that determination to achieve victory, in paying tribute to the sacrifices the RAF had made.

But there was more to the speech than the desire to reflect upon the herculean efforts of the RAF. It also contained a significant passage on the USA and Britain, and the strategic alliances that were being strengthened between the two powers.

Churchill had believed that by bringing America into the conflict, that Germany could be defeated, and he was keen to foster closer ties: "Some months ago," he told Parliament, "we came to the conclusion that the interests of the United States and of the British Empire both required that the United States should have facilities for the naval and air defense of the Western Hemisphere against the attack of a Nazi power… We had therefore decided spontaneously, and without being asked or offered any inducement, to inform the government of the United States that we would be glad to place such defense facilities at their disposal by leasing suitable sites in our transatlantic possessions for their greater security against the unmeasured dangers of the future…"

The detail of the deal that was struck provided Britain with 50 old but vital American destroyers. But it was Churchill's strategic thinking that was more significant, and a

■ **ABOVE: A police officer salutes as Prime Minister Winston Churchill leaves 10 Downing Street in London, August 20, 1940. Churchill was on his way to the House of Commons where he was to make a comprehensive statement on the war situation.**

reflection of his careful calculation. Just a week after taking office as PM, he had confided to his son. "I think I see my way through... I mean we can beat them," he told Randolph. When asked how, Churchill replied, "I shall drag the United States in."

It would be over a year before the Americans were "dragged in," but Churchill appreciated the realities of global conflict on an unprecedented scale. He had seen how the outcome of the war could not be decided by "The Few".

Chapter Eleven:

The End of the Beginning

■ ABOVE: **Franklin D. Roosevelt.**

"We were all united in the great task of ensuring our national survival."

– Clement Attlee

The United States had always held a special place in the heart of Churchill. His mother was American and his frequent visits across the Atlantic had fostered an admiration for US democracy and enterprise. While he was devoted to the British Empire, he realized that Britain and her colonies alone could not defeat the Axis powers.

In America, President Franklin D. Roosevelt had negotiated a tricky course in his nation's relationship to the conflict. Many in the States were ferocious in their opposition to America joining another European war and powerful voices, including Joseph Kennedy, ambassador to London, had written Britain off as doomed. Roosevelt, however, offered support and material aid, exemplified by Lend Lease which came into force in March 1941, providing vital shipping, arms, and supplies on a vast scale to the UK and other beneficiaries, including the Soviet Union.

It was desperately needed. If Britain was to survive, it had to keep its supply line to the US open, and bring in allies to wage war on a number of fronts. The Japanese attack on Pearl Harbor on December 7, 1941 – the day that Roosevelt memorably declared would go down in "infamy" – ended any lingering opposition in America for non-isolation. Now committed to the fray, the US joined the Allied effort that turned the tide of the conflict. The day of Pearl Harbor, Churchill could barely contain his excitement: "We have won the war!"

His relationship with Roosevelt was key. When Tobruk was captured by the vaunted Field Marshal Erwin Rommel in June 1942 during the see-saw British campaign against the Axis in North Africa, Churchill is reported to have cried; Roosevelt, sharing the conference table when the news broke, gave staunch moral and practical support.

The pair met on numerous

■ **ABOVE: Roosevelt and Churchill meet in the mid-Atlantic to agree their war aims, embodied in the Atlantic Charter, 1941.**

occasions and enjoyed a close relationship. They had seen each other for the first time in August 1941 and, after Pearl Harbor, Churchill spoke to a joint session of Congress. Winston's lifelong enthusiasm for America had not always been reciprocated, but that year *Time* magazine made the PM their Man of the Year as the "savior of his country."

The winner the year before was Josef Stalin. When the Germans attacked the Soviet Union in the spring of 1941, it was another turning point in the conflict and brought about an unlikely alliance between the old capitalist, imperialist power, and the emerging totalitarian superpower. Churchill loathed communism with a passion; at home he had wanted to outlaw the British Communist Party at a time when there were calls for a ban on the socialist newspaper the *Daily Worker*. Yet he viewed Nazism as a greater evil and appreciated the need to work with the Russians to defeat Hitler. On a personal level, Stalin and Churchill even got on largely well.

At home, too, political differences were put to one side in the coalition government. Churchill provided effective leadership not just in his own handling of affairs but in marginalizing some of the appeasers (though he embraced and involved some, such as Lord Beaverbrook, who had been admiring of Hitler in the 1930s) and bringing in politicians to government from all sides who could work together. Clement Attlee, leader of the Labour Party, and Herbert Morrison were among those who joined the cabinet. In peacetime they would be in direct opposition but, at a time of war, they were united in a common goal.

As PM, Churchill swept through government like a hurricane. He transformed the business of day-to-day administration, creating an efficient war machine in which people worked long hours and with little rest. It was energetic, dynamic, and imbued with a sense of vitality and purpose – a mirror image of his own style of working. He drove his close supporting officers, such as Ismay, hard, and would antagonize and rankle on a near-daily basis. Not all took to his manner, including senior members of the military. But Churchill was determined to lead a

General Bernard Montgomery as commander of the 8th army and the impact was marked. By November, Rommel's Afrika Korps was on the run and at last Britain had a battlefield triumph over the previously

LEFT: **The Japanese High Seas Fleet launches a devastating, unannounced attack on the American Fleet at Pearl Harbor. They sank six top-line battleships, and hundreds of smaller vessels were either sunk or badly damaged, December 1941.**

BELOW: **A German Panzer III crewman lifts his hands in surrender to an advancing British soldier during the battle of El Alamein, 1942.**

civilian government that ran the war – not the generals, admirals, and air marshals, a legacy of his experience in the First World War. The PM's power was all-encompassing, bolstered by his decision to operate as Minister for Defence.

It helped him to survive his first year in charge and beyond. Despite the USA and the USSR joining the Allies, the progress of the war was not good. Japan was rolling back the British Empire in the east; German panzers made astonishing advances deep into the Soviet Union and were within sight of Moscow; the Battle of the Atlantic was being lost as U-boats inflicted terrible damage on those vital convoys bringing badly needed supplies, so severely that the press was ordered not to publish lists of losses. Churchill had to survive a number of votes of confidence in Parliament – with comfortable majorities, as it transpired – but he sorely needed military victories if his honest but idealistic promises to the British people were to be realized.

Relief was at hand as the Americans halted and turned Japanese expansion in the Battle of Midway. Vindication for Churchill's call to arms came with victory at El Alamein in the fall of 1942. Outraged by successive failures in North Africa, Winston had installed

■ ABOVE: **Prime Minister Winston Churchill and Premier Josef Stalin are shown at one of their meetings in Moscow on August 18, 1942.**

unvanquished Wehrmacht.

It was a symbolic and morale-boosting victory, and Churchill ordered church bells to ring in celebration for the first time since the war had begun. There were to be long years of bitter fighting yet, but typically, Churchill eloquently summarized the situation. At a function held by the Lord Mayor of London, he announced, "This is not the end. It is not even the beginning of the end. But it is, perhaps, the end of the beginning."

Chapter Twelve:

Finest Hours, Declining Powers

ABOVE: Churchill's "V for Victory" sign became a symbol of British history and resiliance.

Churchill had led the country through the most testing of times between 1940-42. His role as Prime Minister enabled him to have a prominent and tangible effect on world events, but his standing was also a symbolic one. Such a divisive figure before the war, he became a unifying personality during it and represented the British people – an island people – as a proud body of men and women standing up for the principles of freedom. He toured the country in the midst of the Blitz and, while he was not universally welcomed by those with who he had little in common, he did not shy from seeing for himself the consequences of what those people suffered from bombing in London, Liverpool, Coventry, and elsewhere. His "siren suits" – effectively one-piece "romper suits" made by Clemmie, and defiantly worn for obvious comfort and practicality – presented him as charmingly eccentric. His famous "V for Victory" sign was turned into a propaganda coup and became a lasting image of the age.

Churchill was influential further afield too. He much admired Canada and on a visit in 1929 wrote: "I am greatly attracted to this country. I have only been here for two days but already I understand why my grandfather was drawn to the beauty and warmth of Canada." He may not have felt quite so fondly about every corner of the "global map colored pink," but even where British dominance was so despised, he rallied colonies and dominions to the flag.

■ **ABOVE: Churchill, framed in the doorway of the historic East Block of the Parliament Buildings, in Ottawa, Canada, February 17, 1942. Churchill is seen entering to attend a special meeting of the war committee of the Canadian cabinet, accompanied by W.L. Mackenzie King.**

"It was the nation and the race dwelling all round the globe that had the lion's heart; I had the luck to be called upon to provide the roar."

– Winston Churchill, on the British people during the Second World War

Australians, South Africans, Indians, Africans, and many more all fought for the Crown, and tens of thousands made the ultimate sacrifice. The British Empire may have been weakening as the conflict progressed but it was making a collective stand against German and Japanese tyranny.

To this end, Churchill was tireless in his efforts to negotiate, cajole, and harangue allies into action. He also sought to pursue British interests within a broad alliance ranged against the European fascist dictatorships and Japanese imperial expansion. He took arduous and dangerous journeys by sea and air to America, the USSR, and North Africa. On one trip to Moscow he traveled 10,000 miles via a circuitous route in extreme conditions – at the age of 67. His health suffered as a consequence and he had bouts of pneumonia and a relatively mild heart attack, but his energy rarely flagged.

That personal drive was needed during the tumultuous year of 1943. In January, the Germans were defeated at Stalingrad: of all the many turning points in the war arguably the most pivotal, for it led to the collapse of Nazi ambitions in the east from which they never recovered. Closer to home, in May, the Battle of the Atlantic had turned in the Allies' favor thanks to a combination of long-range bombers, navy escorts and, crucially, the work of code breakers at Bletchley Park, the British government's monitoring and decryption center, who had broken Germany's "Ultra" codes. Churchill recognized how important this aspect of warfare was and described Bletchley as the "goose that laid golden eggs."

The same month as the Kriegsmarine effectively surrendered at sea, Axis land forces in North Africa also succumbed to the British and American onslaught and the sheer weight of arms and men. Decisions now needed to be made within Allied high command as to where to take the fight to Germany next. Stalin and the Russians had long been pushing for a second front to relieve the pressure on the USSR. America and Britain had their own ideas and it revealed tensions between supposedly united allies.

With the Soviets crushing the Wehrmacht in the titanic Battle of Kursk in July, the stakes were raised. The Germans were in full retreat and, though the war was not yet won, already eyes were on the post-war prize. Roosevelt was, naturally, intent on securing US interests, Stalin and the Soviet Union likewise. Churchill sought to cling on to Britain's empire via the defense of Suez, North Africa, and the Mediterranean. To that end, while American commanders looked to an attack on German-occupied Europe via France, Churchill pushed for an offensive via the "soft underbelly" of Italy, a route that also offered the prospect of cutting across the Soviet advance.

Churchill got his way, and in July Sicily was invaded and Mussolini swiftly deposed. Winston had seen off one dictator and had his eyes firmly set on another but, with the Germans rescuing Mussolini and installing him as nominal leader in the north, they turned the battle for Italy into a long and bloody war of attrition.

The Americans were, meanwhile, fighting on a vast and heroic scale in the Pacific. Heavy bombing of Germany by the British and US air forces was a practical demonstration of the leader of RAF Bomber Command Arthur Harris's guarantee that Germany would reap the whirlwind of her aggression in 1940-41. But the pressure for another army assault in the west was building. At the second Teheran Conference in November 1943, Stalin played a deft diplomatic hand and prevailed. The outcome suited the Americans; less so Churchill. He was a reluctant convert to the idea. He was haunted by the memory of his own strategic blunder, Gallipoli in the First World War. Now he feared casualty rates of 50% among the first wave of troops to land on D-Day.

BELOW: Prime Minister Winston Churchill inspects his old regiment, the 4th Royal Hussars, lined up in front of their tanks, in the Egyptian Desert, near Cairo, in December 1943.

Churchill's misgivings were to be proved misplaced. The nature of Allied power in June 1944, however, showed how his concerns for Britain's status were merited. It was not a British officer in command of Supreme Headquarters Allied Expeditionary Force, or SHAEF. It was an American, General Dwight D. Eisenhower, and it was the Americans and Russians now calling the shots. Britain and her leader were not quite marginalized, but their diminishing status was rendered clear.

ABOVE: Churchill described Bletchley Park as "the goose that laid golden eggs."

LEFT: After an informal luncheon party on Christmas Day to celebrate his recovery from a severe case of pneumonia, Prime Minister Winston Churchill, dressed in his siren suit and dressing gown, was photographed with his guests in Carthage, which included a number of Allied chiefs of staff: Major General J.F.F Whitely (Deputy Chief of Staff), Air Marshal Tedder (Deputy Supreme Commander under General Eisenhower), Admiral Sir John Cunningham (Commander in Chief Mediterranean), General Dwight Eisenhower (Supreme Allied Commander of the British and US Expeditionary Forces in the UK for the liberation of Europe), General Alexander (Commander in Chief of the Allied Armies in Italy), Churchill, Lieutenant General Sir Humfrey Gale (Chief Administrative Officer AFHQ), General Sir Henry Maitland Wilson (Supreme Commander of the Mediterranean Theatre) and General Smith (Chief of Staff at AFHQ), as well as some unnamed members of the military, 1943.

Chapter Thirteen:
Victory in Europe, Defeat at Home

"God bless you all. This is your victory! It is the victory of the cause of freedom in every land. In all our long history we have never seen a greater day than this. Everyone, man or woman, has done their best. Everyone has tried."

– **Winston Churchill**

When the D-Day Armada was launched across the English Channel on June 6, 1944, King George VI had an unlikely if vital task. It was the monarch who finally had to order a reluctant Prime Minister to agree that he could not journey with the first wave of troops assaulting the Normandy beaches.

Winston was, at the age of nearly 70, determined to be on the frontline, both literally and metaphorically. The realities of world politics and the shifting balance of power amid the turmoil of global war meant that British influence was in decline, but Churchill was as busy as ever at the heart of the conduct of the war and the maneuvering for the uncertain peace that was to come.

He eventually got his wish to see the battle in Normandy for himself on June 12, 1944, and was thrilled when the guns of the ship on which he made the voyage, HMS *Kelvin*, opened fire on German positions. He may not have been the most enthusiastic supporter of Operation Overlord but, in tribute to his immense standing, the artificial Mulberry harbor at Arromanches that enabled vital supplies to be landed to fuel the campaign was named in his honor. The war was far from over however. To remind the Premier of the dangers he and his fellow Britons were still exposed to, on the day he returned to London the first "V1" bombs fell on the capital.

The battle for France was marked by disagreements and rivalries

■ OPPOSITE & ABOVE: **Churchill crossed the Channel in the British destroyer *Kelvin* to visit the Normandy landing beaches. The Prime Minister stood on the bridge of the destroyer while she was bombarding enemy positions on the French coast from close range. He was greeted by General Montgomery and received a great welcome from troops unloading stores on the beach. For seven hours he remained in France, driving inland in a jeep toward the battlezone and paying visits to different Allied units throughout his trip. The Prime Minister, seated on the destroyer and wearing sunglasses, watches with interest as the destroyer passes through the varied collection of ships at the bridgehead, in Normandy, France, on June 12, 1944.**

within Allied leadership. Churchill had to play a careful balancing act – defending his senior officers, dealing with the frustrating Free French commander, General De Gaulle, keeping onside with the Americans, and maintaining a wary eye on the Soviets. His enduring fear of communism compelled him to fly to Greece on Christmas Day in 1944 – much to Clementine's upset – to steer difficult negotiations toward an outcome whereby the communists were deprived of control in post-war Greece.

The war continued toward its defining conclusions. Paris was liberated in August, while the Red army wrought terrible vengeance on the Germans for their crimes in the east. By August, the Soviets were in Poland – and here lay one of the central issues that exposed the fundamental challenge for the Allies. The map of Europe was being redrawn. With the two sides – capitalist west and communist east – ideologically opposed, the alliance between the two was already showing signs of fracture.

The protagonists convened at Yalta, in the Crimea, in February 1945. The horse-trading over the composition of Europe and other regions between the major powers at this history-defining

conference caused lasting bitterness. Critics in particular were incensed by the decision to effectively hand over Poland to the Soviets. The situation meant that many of the Poles who had fought bravely for the British during the war would not be returning home to rebuild a Poland according to their wishes, but one under effective Soviet control. Dozens of officers and men even committed suicide in protest.

Churchill's part in Yalta was nuanced and more complex than the face-value impression of him simply agreeing to Russian demands. He tried repeatedly to warn Roosevelt of the threat Stalin posed, but the President's health was waning and his desire for a clear settlement, rather than the prospect of leaving US troops in Europe to deal with the messy aftermath of victory, meant Churchill's view did not hold sway. The conference was billed as the meeting of the "Big Three" but, in reality, it was the "Big Two" with Britain as a supporting act. "Never could I be content with any solution that did not leave Poland a free and independent state," Churchill said, but his hopes were to be abruptly dashed.

The PM was also facing challenges at home. The coalition government had held together well but, with one eye on the peacetime era, ministers were asserting a growing concern for the way the government was led. Clement Attlee, the Deputy Prime Minister in effect, wrote a letter to Churchill criticizing his lack of attention in reading briefing documents and his habit of conducting political business with figures such as Lord Beaverbrook and Brendan Bracken at the Ministry of Information, thus undermining the role of the cabinet.

ABOVE: Winston Churchill with Franklin D. Roosevelt and Josef Stalin at the Yalta Conference, February 4 to 11, 1945.

The criticism stung but it hit home – even Clementine agreed with Attlee's points.

Further controversy was to come in the aftermath of the bombing of Dresden in February 1945. British heavy bombers were by now conducting a strategy of area nighttime bombing of German cities, followed by daylight US raids, with the aim of bringing the whole country to its knees. Such indiscriminate attacks resulted in dreadful civilian casualties – an estimated 25,000 were killed in Dresden alone – and fierce criticism of Churchill at the time and in later years, when it was frequently described as a war crime. Churchill himself recognized the gravity of the situation, noting, "[it] remains a serious query against the conduct of Allied bombing."

Yet, despite these concerns, and the military setbacks at Arnhem and

■ **ABOVE: Flying Fortresses are seen as they drop their bombs over German communication lines at Chemnitz, near Dresden, on February 6, 1945.**

■ **BELOW: The demolished city of Dresden is shown after the Allied forces air raids on February 13 and 14, 1945; up to 25,000 people – perhaps even more – were killed.**

in the Ardennes, the momentum for Allied victory was unstoppable. On May 7, Germany surrendered. The next day was Victory in Europe day, and Churchill took the acclaim of vast celebratory crowds in London. "This is your victory," he announced to the thousands gathered in Whitehall. It was also of course his, and he was reminded by the crowd.

Yet in the moment of triumph, defeat was at hand for Churchill. In the General Election of July 1945, he was utterly trounced at the polls. The perception among voters was that while Churchill was the ideal war leader, a different kind of government was needed in peacetime. Returning servicemen and their wives had wanted to avoid the dashed hopes of their parents who had been promised a "land fit for heroes" after the Great War only for many to find strife and unemployment in peacetime.

The promise of the Welfare State, and in particular the National Health Service, as contained in the Beveridge Report, was supported by Churchill and the Conservatives but not as convincingly as Attlee and the Labour Party, and their majority of 145 seats reflected the change in mood and perspective. Social reform was demanded and, while Churchill had been seen as a reformer in his early Parliamentary career, he was now

perceived as one of the old guard and belonging to a different time. "Let us face the future," was the Labour Party's message. Churchill seemed to many to represent the past, particularly in his campaigning that even drew comparisons of a potential Labour administration with the Gestapo.

It was a view out of step with the times. He had already lost a close friend when Roosevelt died in April. He enjoyed good relations with Roosevelt's successor, Harry Truman, but the world was changing before his and everybody else's eyes. The dropping of the atom bomb on Hiroshima and Nagasaki in August ended the Second World War but signified a new and potentially even more destructive danger than the one Churchill had played such a crucial part in overcoming.

■ **LEFT & ABOVE: At 3pm on May 8, 1945, Prime Minister Winston Churchill announced that the war in Europe would end at midnight. London erupted into a massive chorus of jubilation and celebration. Churchill was greeted by huge cheering crowds wherever he went, and the King was kept busy by a crowd outside Buckingham Palace who made him keep returning to the balcony to receive their accolades. Even his own daughters, escorted by Palace guards, joined the crowd in shouting for the King. All licensing laws in the capital were revoked for the evening and the celebrations went on well into the small hours.**

■ **BELOW: Clementine Churchill laughs heartily as Prime Minister Winston Churchill talks at Chigwell, during his election campaign, May 27, 1945.**

Chapter Fourteen:

The Last Victory

ABOVE: **Winston Churchill speaks at Westminster College in Fulton, Missouri. This was the speech in which he used the phrase "the Iron Curtain," referring to the Soviet occupation of much of eastern Europe.**

"From Stettin in the Baltic to Trieste in the Adriatic, an Iron Curtain has descended across the continent."

– Winston Churchill

Acting "magnanimous in victory" had long been a Churchill maxim – a lesson learned from the experience of the Allies' punishing treatment of Germany after the First World War that directly contributed to the Second. Thus, he was reciprocally gracious in his own election defeat. "The decision of the British people has been recorded. I have therefore laid down the charge which was placed upon me in darker times... It only remains for me to express to the British people my profound gratitude for the unflinching support which they have given me during my task and for the many expressions of kindness which they have shown towards their servant."

That typically lyrical comment may have seemed like a tender parting gift, but if anyone thought Churchill was stepping out of the limelight and meekly into retirement they were mistaken. While he and his party may have been at odds with the British electorate, he had a full and frank contribution to make to international affairs.

He advocated and campaigned for European integration and accord, while distancing himself from the idea that Britain would be part of any new continental order – "We are with Europe, but not of it," was his telling phrase. Instead, Churchill sought to forge even stronger ties between Britain and America. He was absent from the Potsdam Conference between July and August 1945, with his successor Attlee taking his place, but Winston had much to say on the redrawing of the world map and the growing tensions between east and west.

His contribution to the debate was seminal. On March 5, 1946, he was introduced by President Truman to speak at Westminster College in Fulton, Missouri. After declaring his commitment to unity between the English-speaking peoples of America, Britain, and her empire – the "Anglosphere" as Churchill dubbed it – he turned his attention to the situation in Eastern Europe.

If it didn't promote the optimism of his memorable wartime speeches, it did carry the gravitas. Churchill's gift for oratory once again helped to define the age, providing the instantly recognizable image of the state of world affairs. This was the nuclear age and, with the Second World War just won, the survivors faced the very real prospect of mutually assured destruction. While he supported peace talks, Churchill was predictably unequivocal as to where he stood in the wider showdown between capitalism and

ABOVE: **Winston Churchill and President Truman wave from the President's special train as they head for Fulton. In the background is Brigadier General Harry Vaughan, the President's military aide.**

BELOW: **Churchill and Clementine arrive at a pre-election service at St. Paul's Cathedral in London, 1950.**

■ **ABOVE: Churchill pictured with Lord Woolton, during the General Election, 1950.**

communism. He backed Truman to the hilt, judging him "the type of leader the world needs when it needs him most."

The blunt assessments Churchill declared in public did not go down well with many in the west, even if they shared his view. Similarly, his opposition to the break up of the British Empire and, in particular, his misgivings about Indian independence painted Churchill as an outspoken and uncompromising figure. Later still, in the 1950s, he was fearful of immigration: the staunch proponent of the Empire was not happy about the Empire's people coming to live in the mother country.

There were lighter moments as well, though, during his period as leader of the Opposition. During the war, the King had made Churchill the Lord Warden of the Cinque Ports, an ancient ceremonial role rooted in England's medieval past. Given the rather more pressing concerns during the war, Churchill was not able to take up the post so, in August 1946, the investiture took place. Churchill the deposed politician was warmly greeted as Churchill the victorious war hero amid a ceremony of broad pomp and circumstance.

If it seemed like a relic of a bygone age, Churchill showed he could still thrive in the modern era. While Labour had been swept to power on a wave of hope for a better and brighter tomorrow, the reality of the immediate post-war years hit hard. Britain was virtually bankrupted by the conflict, and years of austerity damaged Attlee's ageing administration. Great strides in social reform were made and Britain, with major industries nationalized, was a different country to the one Churchill knew before the war; rationing continued and in some cases was even tightened. In the election of 1950, Labour's majority was slashed. Attlee called another poll to try and boost his majority but, instead, despite winning the popular vote, suffered defeat by a 17-seat margin.

It was Winston Churchill, 76 years old, who would step through the door of No. 10 Downing Street again – this time as Premier once more.

■ **ABOVE: Winston Churchill at Chartwell.**

Chapter Fifteen: Churchill's Twilight Years

■ ABOVE: **Prime Minister Winston Churchill, holding familiar cigar, leans from a train window at Gare du Nord, Paris, France, to bid goodbye to French Defense Minister Georges Bidault and Foreign Minister Robert Schuman. Churchill was leaving the French capital after conferences with other Western Europe leaders.**

"As an old parliamentarian I was rather astonished that something well over £100 million could be disbursed without Parliament being made aware of it."
– Winton Churchill, on Britain's development of a nuclear bomb

Churchill's second tenure proper at No.10 saw him take office at a new juncture of British politics. The consensus era had begun and broad agreement on fundamental policy made the distinctions between Tory and Labourite leadership somewhat indistinct.

Known for his outspoken and maverick ways, it might have been expected for Winston to feel ill-at-ease with this mainstream unity. Instead the PM, perhaps *slightly* mellowed by age, fitted into the spirit of the early 1950s. Times may still have been tough, and Britain was still some way from the land where people had "never had it so good" as one of his successors, Harold Macmillan, would later claim. But with his team of ministers, secretaries, and advisers installed Churchill was firmly at the helm as his administration introduced various domestic reforms such as the Mines and Quarries Act of 1954, and the Housing Repairs and Rent Act a year later, which improved housing standards.

Indeed, the Conservative government embarked on a project of extensive civic house building, promising to build 300,000 new homes per year. Abroad, the situation was less positive. British foreign policy was challenged by the inevitable upheavals of an empire in a long but inexorable decline. The independence movements in Kenya and Malaya were met with direct military interventions and prompted bitter exchanges of violence and the final repressive response of the colonial power. The empire Churchill was so devoted to for so long was withering before his eyes.

There were similar disappointments in the Cold War. The two great adversaries of America and the USSR did not come to direct blows, but the temperature in the relationship between the two was heating up. The nuclear arms race threatened the fragile peace and Churchill could

■ **ABOVE: British Prime Minister Winston Churchill spreads his arms wide as he makes a point in addressing a joint session of Congress in Washington, 1952.**

do little to cool the situation. He made frequent transatlantic trips and was a prime mover in forging the "special relationship" between Britain and the US, but did not enjoy the close and fraternal relationship with President Eisenhower that he had with Roosevelt and then Truman. Indeed, far from putting an end to the arms race, Britain joined it, becoming a nuclear power in 1952 after a successful test off the coast of Australia. The US did not share its nuclear technology with its close ally.

At a time when NATO had been formed (Churchill's old Chief of Staff General Ismay was the organization's first Secretary General) and the Korean War was being fought with the participation of almost 100,000 British troops, the earnestly held belief for peace in the post-Second World War era had come to little. Churchill is famously reported to have said in 1954 "to jaw-jaw is always better than to war-war." But the reality of the international situation was potentially devastating. He gave the go-ahead for the development of Britain's hydrogen bomb, believing that such awesome weaponry would be a deterrent to a kind of war too horrific to contemplate.

These were testing times for any man. For one who was well into his seventies, they were even more of a challenge. For all his energy and enthusiasm, Churchill's physical powers were understandably waning. He was as busy as ever with his writing and penned his six-volume work *The Second World War*. His skills as a writer were acknowledged with the award of the Nobel Prize for Literature in 1953, to follow his knighthood in 1952 bestowed by the new monarch, Queen Elizabeth II.

Time was catching up with him, however. His health problems had surfaced during the Second World War, including a minor heart attack, and stroke in 1945, but they had not seriously hindered his ability to work. By the 1950s however, his ability to recover was significantly diminished. In June 1953, at the age of 78, he suffered a series of more serious strokes at his office in 10 Downing Street. The news was kept quiet, both from Parliament and the nation. Instead, his absence was officially put down to exhaustion.

He convalesced at Chartwell and was able to return to office in October. But the future was clear and his retirement inevitable. In 1955, Churchill stepped down as Prime Minister, to be replaced by the man long regarded as his heir, Anthony Eden (married in 1952 to Churchill's niece Clarissa). Eden's mentor was to remain a Member of Parliament until 1964, but his time at the forefront of British political life was effectively at an end.

■ **ABOVE:** A portrait of Sir Winston Churchill painted by Graham Sutherland and presented to Sir Winston on his 80th birthday by past and present members of the Houses of Lords and Commons, November 30, 1954.

Chapter Sixteen:

Death of a Statesman

■ **ABOVE: Prime Minister Sir Winston Churchill greets crowds at Westminster for his 80th birthday celebrations.**

On November 30, 1954, Churchill celebrated his 80th birthday in the 11th-century Westminster Hall, the oldest building in the grounds of Parliament. The occasion drew warm tributes from across the world of politics, even from those who were regarded as his strident opponents. Clement Attlee, his sometime colleague and later his adversary, described him as "the last of the great orators who can touch the heights." The BBC reported that Churchill received a number of gifts from around the world, including a bouquet in the shape of a cigar from Israel and a sixpenny postal order from a schoolboy from Herefordshire, paid for from his pocket money.

The birthday greetings were a reflection of Churchill's immense standing. As he entered the last years of his career, his status as a giant of British and indeed world history was assured. He had seen extraordinary changes during his lifetime and been party to remarkable events. Now he was seeing out his days in a world far removed from the one he had been born into.

The 80th-birthday ceremony was televised, an indication of the revolutionary technological and social changes of the modern era. Churchill was perhaps not quite a relic of a bygone age, but he was a child of the 19th century, when the nation was indeed a very different country. His time and, to a large extent, his outlook, had passed and, though he continued to live a productive and active life, his later years were more those of reflection and looking back rather than forward.

His writing continued with finishing the epic *A History of the English-Speaking Peoples*, its four volumes published between 1956-58. He spent more time painting at his beloved Chartwell and less time in Parliament as a backbencher. The majority in his seat of Woodford fell at the 1959 General Election and he finally stood down in 1964. In the interim, spells of depression – his "black dog" – wore him down mentally as his physical strength began to falter. Family life was mixed. There were disputes with his son Randolph but, he, Clementine, and the rest of the children stood by him as ever. Tragedy was to come, however, when the couple's daughter Diana took her own life in 1963.

That same year, President John F. Kennedy made Churchill an honorary American, but the beneficiary was too frail to attend the ceremony. In January 1965, Churchill suffered a major stroke and this time there was to be no comeback. Winston Leonard Spencer Churchill passed away on January 24, at the ripe old age of 90.

The legacy he left behind was as substantial as any man could hope for. Churchill had wanted to make his mark on the world from an early age and undeniably succeeded. He has been celebrated, studied, and portrayed ever since, with an almost countless number of books, movies, and TV shows. Statues abound, ships, schools, and streets have borne his name. In the BBC's 2002 poll of the greatest Britons, Churchill led the field. He has become an iconic, almost mythical figure.

But what of the real man himself? Throughout his long and

incredible life, he was a divisive, complex character, and a maze of contradictions. He could be ruthless and magnanimous, tough and caring, uncompromising and diplomatic. His actions during the famine that killed up to three million in Bengal during 1943 caused revulsion and accusations of naked racism. Against that he viewed the Amritsar massacre in 1919 as "monstrous." Churchill was loathed in some quarters, loved in others, but even his staunchest enemies could not underestimate his influence and impact.

At that esteemed Westminster Hall gathering in 1954, a new portrait was unveiled of Churchill by the artist Graham Sutherland. The subject did not like it but, perhaps uncharacteristically, he kept polite counsel. It wasn't always so. Churchill could be brutally honest, gratuitously rude, and certainly objectionable. There are many famous examples of his biting wit. One was an exchange with Lady Astor, who is reported to have said: "If I were married to you, I'd put poison in your coffee." To which Churchill replied: "If I were married to you, I'd drink it."

The story is probably not true, but only adds to the legend. His passing during the "Swinging Sixties" was a hugely symbolic sign of a changing world. Given a state funeral, Churchill departed to huge fanfare. The day was televised live to a global audience of up to 350 million with the great and the good in attendance. As Churchill's body was carried up the Thames, dockside cranes were lowered in his honor. Eventually, Churchill was carried on the final journey to his resting place in Bladon churchyard, close to where it all began, at Blenheim Palace.

■ ABOVE: Winston Churchill's state funeral. Churchill died on January 24, 1965, aged 90. For three days, his body lay in state in Westminster Hall in the House of Commons, followed by a military procession to St. Paul's Cathedral with his coffin on a gun carriage and pulled by sailors of the Royal Navy. After the service, his body was taken by boat from Tower Pier to Waterloo Station, on its way to his family's ancestral home in Blenheim Palace in Oxfordshire. In the Commons, where he had spent over six decades, his seat was left vacant.

SELECT SOURCES

BBC
Churchill by Roy Jenkins (Macmillan, 2001)
Churchill: A Study in Greatness by Geoffrey Best (Penguin, 2002)
D-Day The Battle For Normandy by Antony Beevor (Penguin, 2012)
Dictionary of 20th Century World Biography (OUP, 1992)
NY Times
Winstonchurchill.org
World War Two Tweets

"The journey was interesting, and well worth the taking – once."

– Winston Churchill

Introduction

He had one of the most recognizable faces, a voice to match, and during his long life made an impression few men can possibly hope to emulate. Whether in his stirring words or decisive actions, his triumphs and disasters, the setbacks, comebacks, and era-defining contributions, Winston Spencer Churchill bestrode the worlds of politics, culture, and conflict to make him one of those few individuals who not only participate in history but make it.

He began his life determined to live up to the achievements of his illustrious ancestors, yet struggled to emerge from his father's shadow in his early years. His ambition and will to succeed, however, propelled him into living one of the most compelling of all lives.

Churchill's famous "V for victory" hand signal during the Second World War. The fingers would occasionally be reversed – an old English hand gesture that had a rather more insulting meaning!

Icon

Churchill's image and character has been immortalized in print, on television, on canvas, in fiction, documentary, on bank notes, and so much more – including this stamp. It shows him as the First Lord of the Admiralty during the First World War, and was featured in the "Lord Roberts Memorial Fund Stamp Album." Churchill then and now held a fascination for people across the world, and he is sure to play a central part in the pages of history for many years to come.

Statues of Churchill proliferate in Britain and beyond. This is a tribute to the former Prime Minister outside the Churchill Memorial Museum in Bandar Seri Begawan, Brunei.

On the stump, drumming up votes during an election in Waltham Abbey, on the outskirts of London in 1924. Churchill was the consummate politician, but was not tied down by party political discipline. He switched sides numerous times and his views were often out of step with the prevailing policies of his colleagues. Today, Churchill's own views are still fiercely contested and debated by both sides of the ideological divide – his politics were, perhaps, as tricky to pigeonhole as his character.

Warrior

Churchill's gift for oratory came into its own during the Second World War. In the early phases of the conflict, after he had first come to power as Prime Minister, he used his speechmaking skills to perfectly articulate the life-or-death struggle that faced the British people, but also rally the nation. In a series of legendary speeches he offered nothing "but blood, toil, tears, and sweat," would go on to celebrate the bravery of the RAF in winning the Battle of Britain ("the few"), and imagine a time when people would reflect that "this was their finest hour."

His speech in June 1940, after the Dunkirk evacuation, resonated with the words that "we shall defend our island, whatever the cost may be, we shall fight on the beaches, we shall fight on the landing grounds, we shall fight in the fields and in the streets, we shall fight in the hills; we shall never surrender." It made the lead news of every paper, including the Daily Mirror.

This famous image of Churchill toting a Tommy gun was exploited by both his admirers and detractors - either as a sign of his tough-guy characteristics or his belligerence; Axis propagandists in the Second World War used it to caricature him as a gangster.

DAILY MIRROR, Wednesday, June 5, 1940.

Daily Mirror (JUNE 5)

No. 11,385 ONE PENNY

Registered at the G.P.O. as a Newspaper.

WE NEVER SURRENDER

DUNKIRK —LAST MEN GO

THE French Admiralty announced yesterday that the last land and naval forces defending Dunkirk were embarked during the night.

The port had previously been made useless to the Germans.

The French Navy, it was added, had lost in the Dunkirk operations seven destroyers—Jaguar, Chacal, Adroit, Bourrasque, Foudroyante, Ouragan and Sirocco—and the supply ship Niger.

Confirming the completion of the evacuation, a British communique said: "Our losses, though considerable, are small in comparison to those which a few days ago seemed inevitable."

The French communique states:

"Three hundred French warships and merchant vessels of various sizes, with 200 smaller boats, as well as numerous formations of the Naval Air Arm, took part in this operation.

"Most of the crews of our last naval vessels were saved.

3 Admirals Land

"Other ships were damaged, but some have already put to sea again.

In addition to making Dunkirk unusable as a port, the Allied forces destroyed war material which could not be removed.

"When the Germans enter they will find almost nothing," French reports stated.

Three admirals of the French Navy and three French generals arrived at a south-east coast port yesterday with French troops evacuated from Dunkirk. They travelled to London to visit the Admiralty and War Office.

254 KILLED IN PARIS AIR RAID

Death-roll in Monday's Paris air raid was 254, of whom 195 were civilians and fifty-nine soldiers, says the Paris War Ministry. It adds: 652 were wounded—545 civilians, 107 soldiers.

MILITARY objectives in Munich, Frankfort-on-Main and the Ruhr were bombed by Allied warplanes as a reprisal for Monday's raid on Paris, the official Havas Agency announced last night.

It has now been established that twenty-five of the German bombers taking part in yesterday's raid were brought down.

A Berlin report yesterday stated that a "suburb of Munich" was bombed by an Allied plane, and eight people were killed. One bomb, it was stated, hit a factory, causing much damage.

R.A.F. fighters maintained offensive patrols throughout Monday and early yesterday in the Dunkirk area.

In Germany refineries, oil tanks, supply depots and marshalling yards in the Ruhr Valley, Rhenish Prussia and in the neighbourhood of Frankfort were among the important military objectives attacked.

"EVEN if large tracts of Europe fall into the grip of the Gestapo and all the odious apparatus of Nazi rule, we shall not flag or fail. We will go on to the end, and will fight in France, on the oceans and in the air. We will defend our island, whatever the cost, and will fight on the beaches and landing grounds, in the fields and streets and we shall never surrender.

"Even if this island or a large part of it were subjugated, our Empire abroad, armed and guarded by the British Fleet, would carry on the struggle until, in God's good time, the new world, with all its force and men, set forth to the liberation and rescue of the old world."

That proclamation of the unbreakable Allied will to fight on for freedom was made by Mr. Winston Churchill in his speech to the House of Commons yesterday—the greatest speech ever made by a Prime Minister of Britain.

Standing as the staunch embodiment of that will to fight, he declared:—

"I have myself full confidence that if all do their duty, and if nothing is neglected, and the best arrangements made—as they are being made—we shall prove ourselves once again able to defend our island home.

"We shall ride out the storms of war and outlive the menace of tyranny, if necessary for years."

A roar of cheers answered his superb, stark confidence.

"That is the resolve of the Government—every man of it—and that is the will of Parliament, and the nation," said Mr. Churchill.

"The British Empire and the French Republic, linked together in their cause and in their need, will defend to the death their native soil, aiding each other like good comrades to the utmost of their strength."

THESE were other vital points in the Prime Minister's speech (the full report of which begins on page 3):

Thankfulness at the escape of the B.E.F. must not blind us to the fact that what happened in North France and Belgium was a colossal military disaster.

✦ ✦ ✦

We must expect another blow almost immediately.

✦ ✦ ✦

We have more military forces in this country now than ever before. This will not continue. We shall not be content with a defensive war. We shall build up the B.E.F. once again under its gallant Commander-in-Chief, Lord Gort.

✦ ✦ ✦

Meantime we must bring Britain's defences to the height of efficiency.

The Noble Story of Calais

Given an hour to surrender, 4,000 British and French troops, ordered to hold Calais to the end, spurned the demand to give in and kept the German hordes at bay for four days.

Then silence fell on the port.

Thirty unwounded survivors were taken off by the Navy.

This noble story of the heroic defence of Calais is told on page 3.

Pictures of the Evacuation: Pages 8 & 9

IRONSIDES FOR HOME DEFENCE

SMALL bodies of highly mobile and strongly-armed troops—to be called "Ironsides"—are being organised for home defence by General Sir Edmund Ironside, Commander-in-Chief, Home Forces. There will be many hundreds of these formed from the Regular Army.

The War Office, announcing this last night, says that Sir Edmund has sent to each "Ironside" a copy of the following saying by Oliver Cromwell:—

"Your danger is as you have seen: and truly I am sorry it is so great. But I wish it to cause no despondency, as truly I think it will not: for we are British. . . . It's no longer disputing, but out instantly all you can."

The name Ironside, first given to Cromwell himself by Prince Rupert after the battle of Marston Moor in 1644, was later given to the troopers of his cavalry — those "God-fearing men," raised and trained by him in an iron discipline.

It traditionally implies great bravery, strength or endurance.

400,000 Local Defence Volunteers

Lord Croft, Under-Secretary for War, stated in the House of Lords last night that 400,000 had volunteered for the L.D.V.

He protested against suggestions that officers who had come forward were too old.

"It is no mere outlet of patriotic emotion that we are endeavouring to recruit," he said, "but a fighting force which may be at grips with the enemy next week or even to-morrow."

Lord Strabolgi said that besides making open spaces unusable for the landing of invading planes we should do the same with large spaces of water.

Lord Breadalbane suggested that each local area should have a lorry armoured against splinters and bullets and armed with a couple of guns

RUMOUR-MONGER TO BE CHARGED

A CHARGE of being responsible for a rumour that he had heard from a German broadcast by Lord Haw-Haw that the Nazis were going to attack a Mansfield school is being brought today against a man at Mansfield.

This was stated today by Mr. J. L. Nicol, Regional Information Officer, at the inaugural meeting at Nottingham of the North Midland Regional Advisory Committee, which will function under the jurisdiction of the Ministry of Information.

Mr. Nicol added: "A Ministry official will attend."

This will be the first case of its kind under the new regulations.

LIVESTOCK LEAVES COAST

As a precautionary measure, the numbers of livestock in certain areas in South-East England are being reduced, says the Ministry of Agriculture. Some store animals, particularly ewes and lambs, are being transferred to other counties.

Stock fit for immediate slaughter is being bought by the Ministry of Food. The dispersal is not in any way extensive, and will not have any effect upon supplies of home-killed meat in those areas.

Echoing a First World War poster in which Lord Kitchener sternly pointed outward to demand recruits, this no-nonsense rallying cry demanded victory.

Churchill had graduated from Sandhurst in December 1894 and served with the cavalry in India and the Sudan. His military career was relatively short-lived once he entered the political arena, but he returned to uniform in 1915 when he resigned his parliamentary position, and briefly commanded a battalion of the Royal Scots Fusiliers.

Churchill may have been back in civilian clothes in 1940, but he was keen to visit the frontline, in this case inspecting Britain's coastal defenses. Throughout the Second World War, Churchill would undertake hazardous journeys and often had to be dissuaded from getting close to the action.

In July 1945, Churchill visited the location where his deadly enemy had been finally defeated – the bunker in Berlin which was Adolf Hitler's last refuge, and where the defeated Fuhrer took his own life at the end of the Second World War.

Young Adventurer

The young Churchill's taste for excitement and danger had been only partly fulfilled by his spell in military service. As a war correspondent, he traveled to South Africa for a newspaper, filing thrilling dispatches to eager readers back home.

It was Churchill's dramatic capture and subsequent escape from the Boers that truly catapulted him into national renown. He had slipped out of Pretoria and traveled undercover to eventually reach Durban and safety on December 23, 1899. Seven days later, his account of his escapades, entitled "How I Escaped from Pretoria" (along with an article by the Earl of Dunraven, entitled "What 5,000 Horsemen Might Do"), was featured in Pearson's Illustrated War News.

HOW I ESCAPED FROM PRETORIA.

By Winston Churchill.

The *Morning Post* has received the following telegram from Mr. Winston Spencer Churchill, its war correspondent, who was taken prisoner by the Boers and escaped from Pretoria:

LOURENCO MARQUES, December 21st, 10 p.m.

I was concealed in a railway truck under great sacks.

I had a small store of good water with me.

I remained hidden, chancing discovery.

The Boers searched the train at Komati Poort, but did not search deep enough, so after sixty hours of misery I came safely here.

I am very weak, but I am free.

I have lost many pounds weight, but I am lighter in heart.

I shall also avail myself of every opportunity from this moment to urge with earnestness an unflinching and uncompromising prosecution of the war.

On the afternoon of the 12th the Transvaal Government's Secretary for War informed me that there was little chance of my release.

I therefore resolved to escape the same night, and left the State Schools Prison at Pretoria by climbing the wall when the sentries' backs were turned momentarily.

I walked through the streets of the town without any disguise, meeting many burghers, but I was not challenged in the crowd.

I got through the pickets of the Town Guard, and struck the Delagoa Bay Railroad.

I walked along it, evading the watchers at the bridges and culverts.

I waited for a train beyond the first station.

The out 11.10 goods train from Pretoria arrived, and before it had reached full speed I boarded with great difficulty, and hid myself under coal sacks.

I jumped from the train before dawn, and sheltered during the day in a small wood, in company with a huge vulture, who displayed a lively interest in me.

I walked on at dusk.

There were no more trains that night.

The danger of meeting the guards of the railway line continued; but I was obliged to follow it, as I had no compass or map.

I had to make wide *détours* to avoid the bridges, stations, and huts.

My progress was very slow, and chocolate is not a satisfying food.

The outlook was gloomy, but I persevered, with God's help, for five days.

The food I had to have was very precarious.

I was lying up at daylight, and walking on at night time, and, meanwhile, my escape had been discovered and my description telegraphed everywhere.

All the trains were searched.

Everyone was on the watch for me.

Four wrong people were arrested.

But on the sixth day I managed to board a train beyond Middleburg, whence there is a direct service to Delagoa.

WHAT 5,000 HORSEMEN MIGHT DO.

BY THE EARL OF DUNRAVEN.

Without indulging in ungenerous and untimely criticism, one lesson to be learned from the war is, I think, worthy of immediate attention, for it may be put to immediate use. The value of the individual unit, in his capacity to inflict damage and protect himself, is larger in comparison with the value of the collective unit than was the case formerly. The value of rapidity of movement is also enhanced. In other words, the proportionate value of what may be termed regular and irregular troops has altered in favour of the latter.

This shifting of relative values, which certainly is universally true in all war, is accentuated in operations carried on under certain conditions, such as those affecting the present struggle and the many minor wars in which we are frequently engaged. The moral to be drawn is the necessity of creating at home and in the colonies what, for want of a better term, may be called an irregular force—a force of mounted riflemen, men in whom training, rapidity of movement, accurate shooting, ability to take cover, and self-dependence should be primary, and all the admirable qualities comprised under discipline should be secondary considerations.

I should like to see a force of, say, 50,000 mounted sharpshooters raised, 20,000 at home, 10,000 each in Canada, Australasia, and South Africa respectively—a Volunteer force, but liable for foreign service. Its annual training should be short, just enough drill in combined numbers to give the necessary coherence in movement, but its members should be constantly exercised in shooting, not only at fixed targets, but at moving objects.

It should, in fact, be a rifle club of first-rate horsemen, with sufficient drill to enable them to move about, supported, of course, on active service with a little over their complement of regular field artillery. Half of the force would be available for foreign service at a week's notice. I believe such a force could be raised without trenching upon the recruiting for Line, Militia, Yeomanry, or Volunteers, for it would tap a different class of men. That is, I venture to think, a lesson taught by the war to be put into future practice. But the idea can be utilised now. Why are we not availing ourselves of the splendid material existing in Cape Colony and Natal?

It would be easy to raise, equip, and mount 10,000 British, African born. Why is it not done? Man for man they are better than the Boers, superior in fighting qualities, and equal in marksmanship, mobility, knowledge of the country and of Boer modes of fighting. They should be attached to definite divisions, brigades, or smaller commands, and, of course, under the officer commanding, but left entirely free to carry out his instructions in their own way. Consider what even only 5,000 of such men would be to Lord Methuen. They would relieve the tension upon him in a week. Boers are not fighting men who can shoot; they are shooting men who can fight, and who display great courage in their own mode of carrying on war.

Had 5,000, or even half that number, of detached mounted men made a raid upon the main laager during Lord Methuen's last attack the result would have been very different. Though the main attack might have failed, as it did, the Boers would not have waited for another. The Free Staters, at any rate, on the very verge of rupture, would have gone home.

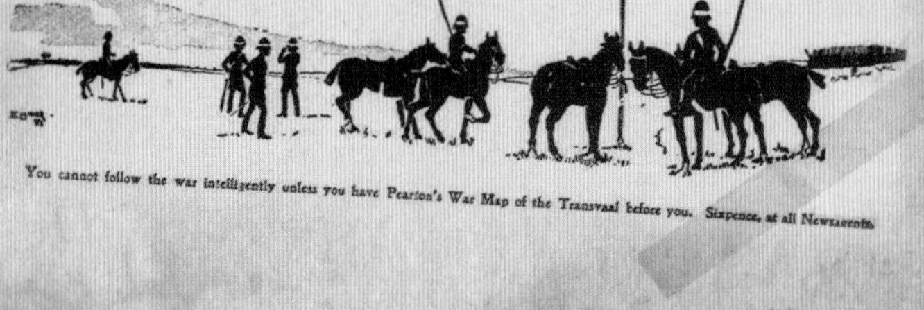

This 1901 portrait showed the young Winston in a rare moment of pause, during his early days as a Member of Parliament. He came from an aristocratic clan and had a lot to live up to – politics would be the arena in which he would really excel.

Ancestors

Winston's most illustrious ancestor was John Churchill, the 1st Duke of Marlborough (1650–1722). He was the commander in chief of the armies of England and Holland in the war of the Spanish Succession, and the victor of the Battle of Blenheim.

A French satirical woodcut of the 1st Duke of Marlborough.

"MALBOROUK."
Illustration, Early Nineteenth Century, to French song (broadside), Bibliothèque Nationale, Paris.

Marlborough's wife was Sarah Jennings (1660–1744). Ambitious and influential at court, she helped to reconcile Anne and William III, smoothing the often-tortuous successions and relationships within the English monarchical system.

Winston's grandfather, John Winston Spencer Churchill (1822–1883), the 7th Duke, was a respected MP representing the Woodstock constituency and also served in Benjamin Disraeli's administrations. He was also Lord Lieutenant of Ireland from 1876 to 1880, where young Winston lived for some time.

Forebears

Winston's mother was the American heiress Jennie Jerome (1854-1921). She would play a pivotal role in his early career, drawing on her high-society connections to aid her son's progress.

Winston's father, Lord Randolph (1849-1895). A complex character, he shared the same ambition and personal drive that his son was to exhibit, but was continually frustrated in his own political career. He and Winston had a difficult relationship – the father was repeatedly disappointed in his son and would regularly chide him for his lack of success and application at school.

ATHWART THE COURSE.

R-ND-LPH CH-RCH-LL (an aggravating Boy). "IN THE WAY AGAIN! 'OORAY!!"

Randolph was often lampooned in the press. This Punch cartoon of July 1883 mocked him for his single-minded determination to steer a different political course to that of his colleagues, and was captioned: (an aggravating boy) – " In the way again! Ooray!!"

Randolph cutting a solitary figure in this Vanity Fair cartoon. He died at the age of just 45.

Family and Childhood

Winston (right) with his mother Jennie and brother John. The two brothers were joined on the frontline in the Boer War, where the younger was injured.

Winston aged five in a sailor suit - a precursor to his time in charge of the Royal Navy.

Harrow School was – and still is – one of the pre-eminent educational institutions for the British ruling elite. Churchill's spell at the school was mixed: while he excelled in some subjects, he was lonely and felt isolated from his parents.

Politician

Churchill at 30, having seen the world in defense of the Empire and then about to embark on his political career.

A scene from the infamous Sidney Street siege, in London's East End in 1911. Churchill was then Home Secretary, and can be seen fourth from the left with a posse of armed policemen. His forthright and uncompromising actions earned him notoriety as well as admiration.

With his distinctive look and voice, Churchill was a godsend for the caricaturists, as with this cartoon from 1913.

Painter, Writer, Thinker

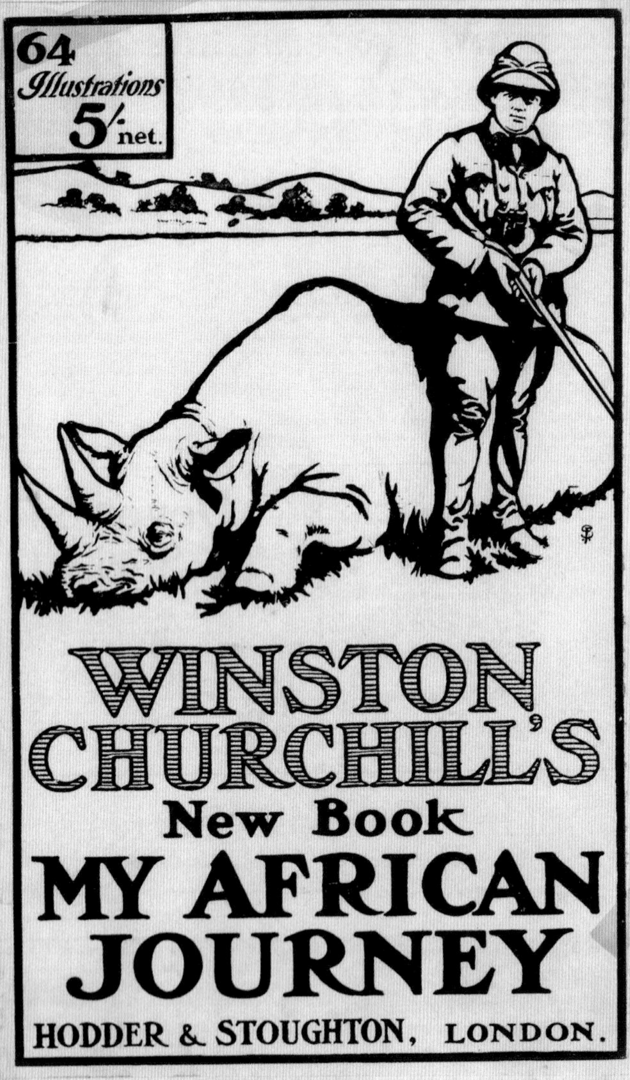

Churchill pursued the craft of writing from an early age – partly out of economic necessity, partly out of his desire to articulate his ideas and opinions. Dictating to hard-worked secretaries and assistants, he wrote prodigiously throughout his adult life, whether in newspaper articles or books, such as 1908's My African Journey, in the course of which he apparently killed a rhinoceros.

Painting was another love of Churchill's life and he was an accomplished artist. On a trip to Miami in 1946, he was pictured with brushes and easel.

Bricklaying was an unlikely Churchillian hobby. He would build walls at his beloved Chartwell and even joined the Amalgamated Union of Building Trade Workers. It has been suggested that the regularity of the technique of laying lines of bricks provided him with quiet moments to reflect on the great affairs of state that weighed heavily on his shoulders, and offered some escape when he was struck by the debilitating periods of depression – the dark moods he described as his "black dog."

Husband

Winston pictured with his wife-to-be, Clementine Hozier, in 1908. Their partnership was long and dependable – his beloved "Clemmie" providing love and calm away from the rigors of public life.

Stepping out in his best dress for marriage to Clemmie on September 12, 1908. That year, Churchill was made President of the Board of Trade.

M. Winston Churchill.

The devoted couple in 1940. They had five children: Diana, Randolph, Sarah, Marigold (who died in infancy), and Mary.

From Insider to Outcast

August 15, 1914] THE SPHERE 183

The MEN who are DIRECTING BRITAIN'S NAVY.

DRAWN BY F. MATANIA

THE FIRST LORD WITH HIS TWO HIGHEST EXECUTIVE OFFICERS

RIGHT HON. WINSTON CHURCHILL—Mr. Churchill is not quite forty years old yet, but he is known throughout the world as a most capable administrator of English affairs. He was first elected for Parliament in 1900 as a Conservative member, but in the year 1906 he was returned for N.W. Manchester as a Liberal. He has been First Lord of the Admiralty since 1911

REAR-ADMIRAL CHARLES MADDEN (second in command) has just relinquished the command of the 3rd Cruiser Squadron of the Home Fleets. He entered the Navy in 1875. He was in command of one of the earliest flotillas of torpedo-boat destroyers in the Mediterranean. He became captain of the original "Dreadnought" in 1907. He has gained a high reputation

ADMIRAL SIR JOHN JELLICOE—Vice-Admiral Jellicoe has just been appointed Commander-in-Chief of the Home Fleet in place of Admiral Callaghan. Admiral Jellicoe has acted since 1912 as Second Sea Lord of the Admiralty. He saw service in China from 1898-1901, when he commanded the Naval Brigade there. He was commander of the Atlantic Fleet during 1910-11

With the advent of the First World War, Churchill, as First Lord of the Admiralty, was prominent in shaping strategy and the conduct of the war. He later regarded it as the most enjoyable period of high office. In this illustration he was pictured deep in contemplation while discussing strategy with Admirals Sir Charles Madden and Sir John Jellicoe.

Churchill was the prime instigator of a British plan to open up a new front in the Mediterranean by attacking Turkey through the Dardanelles at Gallipoli. The original caption for this photograph was "short of ammunition but still they press on, the true bulldog rush of our troops," but behind the naïve patriotism was a bitter truth: the campaign was a disaster for the Allies, and Churchill became the focus of severe criticism.

German satirists swiftly exploited Churchill's fall from grace. He was sacked from the cabinet and even rejoined the army for a brief period.

Zeichnung von F. Jüttner.

Churchill ist zufrieden! Mrs. Britannia hat einen bösen Sturz von ihrem hohen Pferd getan. Aber schon ist ein dummer August da und beruhigt das Publikum!

Outsider

By the 1930s, Churchill was cast out from the political frontline and his better days seemed behind him. In 1933, he was described as a "British statesman and author," when pictured reading correspondence at his desk.

While Germany sank into totalitarianism and prepared for another war, Churchill was one of the louder voices warning of the threat this growing militarization posed. In the Gabriel Gobin in Le Pelerin he was pictured warning neutral nations that if they collaborated with the Axis powers, they were liable to be swallowed up.

Churchill's home life provided some compensation away from the driving seat of world affairs. The family lived at Hoe Farm (above), in Surrey after he first left the admiralty, and Chartwell became the family seat, where Winston would often wear the special siren suits made by Clemmie, once her husband had returned to the forefront of government.

Statesman

THE CONFERENCE AT CAIRO

Conflict inevitably gave Churchill the platform to shape foreign affairs. In 1921, he attended the Conference at Cairo to discuss Mesopotamia (Iraq), alongside the likes of King Faisal of Iraq, Sir Percy Cox, and Gertrude Bell. It was a controversial place and period, when Britain used bombing against civilians to enforce rule. Churchill even went so far as to advocate using poisonous gas against what he called "uncivilized tribes."

Though he was an implacable opponent of communism, Churchill was ready to deal with leaders on the opposite side of the ideological divide. In fact, he and Soviet leader Josef Stalin got on well personally, and were all smiles at the famous Yalta Conference in February 1945.

Churchill was energetic in forging close ties with America and met US President and close ally F. D. Roosevelt in the mid-Atlantic in 1941.

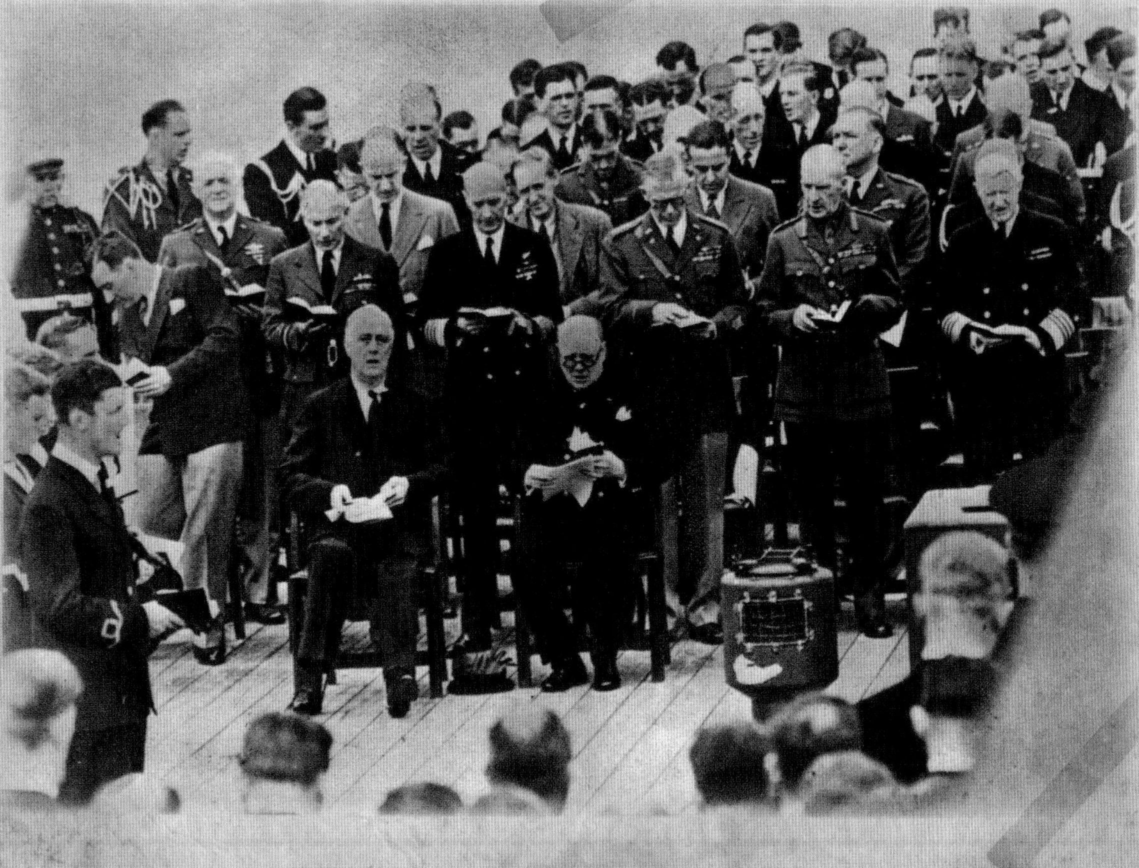

Leader

For the greater part of over half a century, Churchill was in positions of significant power. As First Lord of the Admiralty, he inspected sailors at Chatham, and was kitted out in the finest ceremonial garb.

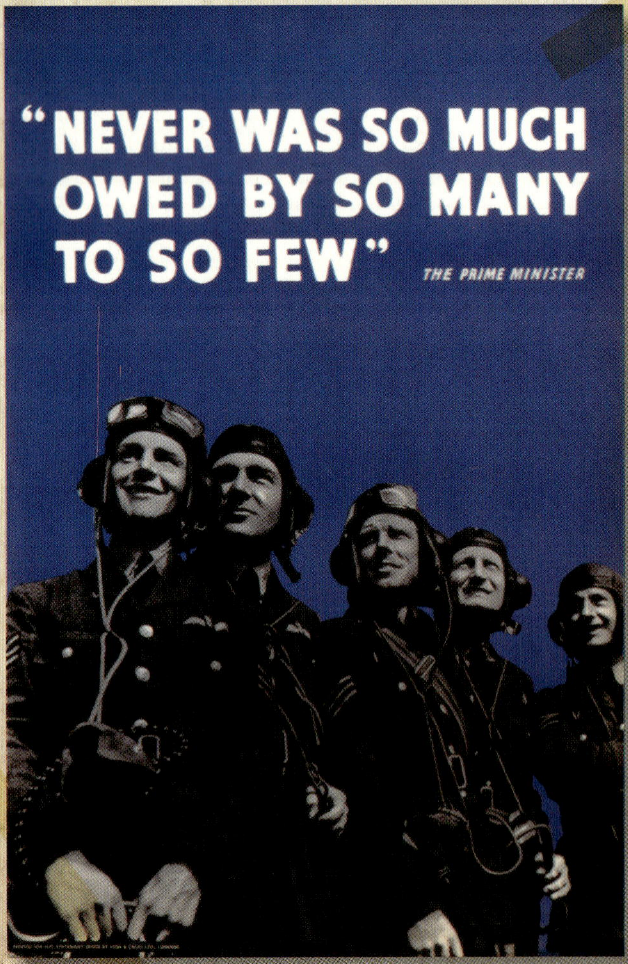

Of all Winston Churchill's famous speeches, "The Few" was arguably the most famous, and was a perfect illustration of his ability to convey strong leadership.

His enemies were keen to undermine Churchill's credentials as a powerful leadership figure, and the Nazis sought to portray him as craven and dependent on America's military muscle.

Twilight Years

By the mid-1950s, the grand old statesman was winding down his long career. He had won another British General Election six years after it seemed he was being consigned to history, but even after being succeeded as Prime Minister, still played a full and active part in public life.

DOMENICA DEL CORRIERE

Anno 67 - N. 4-5 - L. 70 | Settimanale del CORRIERE DELLA SERA | 31 gennaio 1965

CHURCHILL:
un secolo di storia

Da pagina 7: la vita del grande statista raccontata da AUGUSTO GUERRIERO

In death, he was celebrated and acknowledged around the world, including in Italy where La Domenica del Corriere issued a commemorative front cover.

Royalty and statesmen from many nations assembled on the steps of St. Paul's Cathedral in London to pay tribute to the passing of a giant of the 20th century, as he began his final journey to his resting place at Bladon.